# Stories from the Heart

PROJECT SPONSORS
Western Historical Manuscript Collection,
University of Missouri in Columbia

Missouri Folklore Society

Fund for Folk Culture's Artist Support Program underwritten by
The Ford Foundation with additional support from The William and
Flora Hewlett Foundation and The San Francisco Foundation.

SPECIAL THANKS
Claudia Powell, Western Historical Manuscript Collection,
University of Missouri in Columbia

The author thanks the Missouri Arts Council, the State Historical
Society of Missouri Brownlee Fund, and the Artists Support Fund
for Folk Culture for assistance in collecting the stories and preparing
them for publication.

MISSOURI HERITAGE READERS
General Editor, Rebecca B. Schroeder

Each Missouri Heritage Reader explores a particular aspect of the state's rich cultural heritage. Focusing on people, places, historical events, and the details of daily life, these books illustrate the ways in which people from all parts of the world contributed to the development of the state and the region. The books incorporate documentary and oral history, folklore, and informal literature in a way that makes these resources accessible to all Missourians.

Intended primarily for adult new readers, these books will also be invaluable to readers of all ages interested in the cultural and social history of Missouri.

# Other Books in the Series

# Stories from the Heart

## Missouri's African American Heritage

*Collected and Told by Gladys Caines Coggswell*

UNIVERSITY OF MISSOURI PRESS

COLUMBIA

Library of Congress Cataloging-in-Publication Data

Coggswell, Gladys Caines.
  Stories from the heart : Missouri's African American heritage / Collected and Told by Gladys Caines Coggswell.
      p. cm.
  Includes bibliographical references and index.
  Summary: "A collection of African American family stories and traditional tales, compiled and brought to print by a master storyteller as she visited Missouri communities and participated in storytelling events over the last two decades"—Provided by publisher.
  ISBN 978-0-8262-1844-5 (alk. paper)
  1. African Americans—Missouri—Folklore. 2. African Americans—Missouri—Social life and customs. 3. Tales—Missouri. 4. Oral tradition—Missouri. 5. Missouri—Social life and customs. I. Title.
  GR111.A47.C35 2009
  398.2088'960730778—dc22

                                                    2009008543

Designer: Stephanie Foley
Typesetter: FoleyDesign
Typeface: Adobe Caslon

*In memory of Marie Cofer, my great-grandmother, and my mother, Barbara Caines Rice*

*To my aunt Marie White and my sister, Claudia Intsiful*

*To Adele Levine, my dear friend, who believed in me when no one else did and was responsible for my going to college.*

*And to Dana Everts-Boehm, who started me on this journey.*

# Contents

# Foreword

As the director of the Missouri Folk Arts Program, and another transplant to Missouri, I have been honored to know Gladys Coggswell for nine years. She and the folk arts program have had a longer relationship, though, starting back in 1987 when she was an apprentice to renowned St. Louis jazz singer Mae Wheeler in the Traditional Arts Apprenticeship Program. In the early 1990s Gladys emerged as a fully bloomed storyteller, with strong and well-established roots in the oral tradition. A true griot, she does not simply access a catalogue of stories for performances. She has that unerring knack for picking the most relevant piece for any occasion. She excels when she uses stories to teach, to heal, and to enlighten. She is now one of Missouri's foremost storytellers, teaching artists, and community scholars. She has worked tirelessly to preserve, document, teach, and present the artistic, historical, and contemporary cultural significance of the African American story in Missouri. In 2005 she suffered a stroke and really scared us all quite a bit. Thankfully, she has recovered nicely. Gladys has many valuable stories to share, both orally and in the papers she has donated to the archives at the Western Historical Manuscript Collection at the University of Missouri in Columbia. Similarly, with the cooperation of other gifted storytellers, in this book she achieves her goals to preserve, document, and share, planting seeds of knowledge, healing, and truth about African American experiences in Missouri.

Gladys herself has an extensive repertoire, and in the following pages she shares tales from her own life as well as those passed down within her extended family. She has gathered over twenty stories from several regions along the Mississippi River and westward, culling from hundreds of stories she collected through years of field research conducted in African American communities. She started with her neighbors in northeast Missouri, learning the hidden local histories of emancipation and integration in Frankford, Hannibal, and an area near Louisiana, Missouri, known to locals as "Little Africa" and reputed in oral tradition to be a hiding place for runaway slaves that later evolved into an all-black community. Gladys then expanded her field of research, moving from the rolling rural hills of the northeast to the city of St. Louis, a major destination for African Americans during the Great Migration. Her interviews with urban blacks often led her to Missouri's deep south, known in the vernacular as the Bootheel, where cotton and other staple crops were cultivated first by slaves and then by sharecroppers. Understandably a sense of place is central to the stories collected in this volume. Locations convey much more than simple geography. Churches, front porches, schools, and fields provide missing links to the day-to-day lives, personal struggles, and accomplishments of the narrators. Moving toward western Missouri, she found a touching memory of a family rite of passage.

Folklorist Amy Shuman, in *Other People's Stories: Entitlement Claims and the Critique of Empathy,* tells us that stories have consequences and meaning much bigger than an isolated incident experienced by a single person. The stories collected here are truly important to the tellers, their families, and local communities, and the stories will be of immense importance to those of us who have read our U.S. and Missouri history without hearing the voices of ordinary people and their extraordinary lives. Throughout the following pages, readers will find a lush and vivid garden of stories as told to and collected by Gladys Coggswell. Missouri's soil is fertile, and Gladys has planted a variety of perennials that come back season after season, cuttings from neighbors down the way, transplants from a beloved great-grandmother, and seeds from a cherished bloom. Some have deep roots in Missouri while others are more freshly sowed, kind of like Gladys, who is herself a transplant from the mid-Atlantic region of the United States but whose great-grandfather hailed from the Show-Me State.

Lisa L. Higgins
Columbia, Missouri

# Acknowledgments

African in its origin and American in its context and immediacy, the African American traditional story and the legacy of traditional storytelling are very much alive today in the United States, and especially in Missouri. In 1984 the National Endowment for the Arts (NEA) offered funding to states to honor traditional artists and encourage them to pass on their skills—skills they had learned by imitation of respected models in their communities rather than through academic study. Among artists previously honored by the NEA, traditional artists had largely been neglected. In many areas authentic folk arts such as storytelling, fiddling, shape note singing, and jazz tap dance as well as crafts such as johnboat building, all of which once flourished in many Missouri communities, were disappearing. The Missouri Arts Council and the Cultural Heritage Center at the University of Missouri in Columbia developed a state plan to honor and preserve the traditional arts in the state, in part by an innovative program called the Missouri Traditional Arts Apprenticeship Program (MTAAP).

In this program, a statewide panel of experts in traditional arts selects participants, both masters and apprentices, from many applications. The criteria for selection to become a master artist require that the person be part of a community in which the art plays an important role in cultural life and that its practice is in danger of dying out. The master artist's work must demonstrate a traditional form, and he or she must have learned the art within a community where it was practiced. I grew up in a family of storytellers, and while I was serving as a master storyteller in the Missouri Folk Arts Program I soon found that the "apprentices" I worked with are truly the master storytellers. I have learned from them all. They and other community and professional storytellers I have met in Missouri have been an inspiration to me, providing a validation of an approach to culture that allows artists to transcend artificial barriers between people created by man.

Scientists have told us that we are driven by nature or by nurture. The storyteller knows that one without the other is impossible. As generations have found, stories validate our experience, preserve our history, teach valuable life lessons, nurture us, and enrich our creative vision. Some of the stories here are told by native Missourians, others by people like myself for whom Missouri is an adopted home state. Some are told by storytellers who once lived in Missouri but now live across the river in Illinois and come back to Missouri to tell stories in schools, during festivals, or at folklore meetings. All those whose stories are recorded here are African Americans, and their stories reflect not only the struggles endured but the resilience, creative spirit, mother wit, strong sense of family and tradition, hard-won wisdom, and humor in both victory and defeat that distinguish their people.

Some of the contributors to this collection have shared their stories at gatherings, some in a letter to me or during a recorded interview. All have been generous in granting permission for the stories to be published and to be placed in the University of Missouri Western Historical Manuscript Collection in Columbia for future generations. I would like to thank them for honoring me by sharing their eloquent remembrances and traditional stories, all of which provide significant insights into a vital part of Missouri's African American heritage.

I would also like to thank Lisa Higgins and Debbie Bailey of the Missouri Folk Arts Program and David Moore, associate director of the Western Historical Manuscript Collection in Columbia, who have been of great help during the preparation of the book.

Gladys Caines Coggswell
Frankford, Missouri

# Stories from the Heart

# Introduction
# Family Stories

My memories of my own family's storytelling reach back to my great-grandparents. Both told me many stories. My great-grandmother Marie Wallace Cofer disciplined me with stories. If I behaved in a manner that was unacceptable to God and to her, she had a story about a sinful person (or sometimes it was an animal) that had behaved in the same dastardly way I had, and who, of course, came to an extremely bad end. I did not want to come to a bad end, so there were times when I tried very hard to behave.

Once, when she knew I was not telling the truth, she shook her finger in my face and admonished me with a story. We never used the word "lie" or any form of "lie" in our household because my great-grandmother said it was a bad word, and spouting bad words was definitely a sin. So she said, "Girl, you better tell the truth while you can. I heard about a man who fibbed and his head fell off." The head hit the ground and started rolling down the road. It rolled really fast, and by the time it came to a stop it had turned into stone. A little old lady who had been watching stepped up to the stone and asked if it was a head. Of course the head couldn't answer. By the time this happened, stones were no longer able to speak.

My great-grandmother let me know that my head was so hard it

1

Gladys (on the right) and Claudia Caines grew up in Patterson, New Jersey, in the home of their great-grandmother Marie Cofer, who ran a boardinghouse in the city. (Coggswell Collection)

Marie Cofer had a large repertoire of stories, most of which served as lessons for children who misbehaved. (Coggswell Collection)

was close to becoming a stone right then. I was so afraid my head might turn to stone that I told the truth for a long time after that—at least a week. I still try to tell the truth most of the time.

Admittedly, as a young child I didn't always appreciate my great-grandmother, her prayers, or her stories. I can remember thinking, "Why can't she just stop talking and beat me like other people beat their children?" But she would either tell stories or say one- to three-hour prayers, depending on the severity of my sinful behavior. My great-grandmother was a Baptist and known to all for being long-winded. She was a dyed-in-the-wool Christian who walked and talked the straight and narrow.

I remember coming home from school one afternoon, bawling my eyes out, crying to my great-grandmother that I didn't want to be short or fat because the kids were making fun of me. She shook her finger in my face.

"You better hush up that nonsense, girl," she said. "Don't you know everybody is born with a special gift to use to make the world a better place to live in? When people make fun of what is on the outside of you, it's because they don't know what your special gift is. They don't even know what their own special gift is. If they did, they'd be using it instead of laughing at you.

"Listen. If you let other people's stuff into your head, you won't have enough space left to think about what your own special gift is, and then you can't do the work you are here to do. You better start appreciating who and what you are, or you're going to end up like the eagle, with a bald head."

And then she told me the story my great-grandfather had told her about why the eagle has a bald head.

～

There was once a young eagle girl who was very nosy. Every day she went flying around, trying to see who was doing what. Once she went flying along the Mississippi River where Jabo Jones was fishing. Now Jabo was just about the most handsome man she had ever seen. When he raised his head, she almost fell out of the sky. There in his smooth chocolate-brown face was a set of the most beautiful and mysteriously penetrating eyes she had ever seen. Her heart began to beat like a drum, and she flew home to find her father. "Daddy, Daddy," she beseeched him. "I don't want to be an eagle any more. I want to be a young woman, so I can marry that man fishing down by the Mississippi River." Her father was stunned and told her to go rest her wings, for she had surely been in the sun too long. She responded to his advice with a temper tantrum.

Not sure what he should do, he did what any self-respecting father does when uncertainty sets in about handling a sticky situation. He called for her Mama. This time Mama couldn't handle the young eagle either, so she called Grandpa Eagle, who was a no-nonsense kind of a bird. Grandpa Eagle put his wings on his hips, shook his head, and said, "If she doesn't want to be an eagle, let her go." Now since Grandpa Eagle was an elder, he was respected, listened to, and obeyed. Mama Eagle's sniffling and reminding him that this was her baby did not change a thing.

Late that night there was a ceremony. The eagles came from near and far and, joined by a few other curious creatures, made a circle. They all swayed from side to side and sang, "Ummh, Ummh, Ummh, change this eagle into a woman." Bamm! Before anyone could sing another "ummh," there stood a woman where the eagle had once stood. She was so excited that she began to walk off without even saying thank you.

Grandpa Eagle stopped her and said, "Hold on right there, girlie. We couldn't change your talons into human feet, so there are wrappings under your shoes. If anyone would ever see your naked talons, woe be unto you." She didn't care. She had to get to the river, and the man—who totally ignored her when she got there and pranced back and forth in front of him. After all, he was fishing. But she wasn't going to be ignored. She threw a rock in the water. This upset Jabo, who got up intending to say some unkind words. But when their eyes met, he forgot all about fishing and everything else but her. They began to walk, and they began to talk, and then they got married.

They would have lived happily ever after, but Jabo just could not be happy with a woman who never took off her shoes and wrappings. Determined to find out why, he waited until she was asleep one night and then gently, quietly, removed the blanket and then a shoe from one foot. As he quietly went about the business of removing the wrappings, he noticed that the sun was rising and the room was getting lighter. Just as the sun was shining full force into the room, he got the last of the wrappings off, looked down, and screamed. The scream woke his wife. Seeing her talon exposed, she went into spasms and raised her arms, which became eagle wings. Her face took on the form of an eagle's face, and she began to fly away. Her husband grabbed her hair to try to stop her, but she was too powerful for him. She broke right through the glass window and flew high into the sky. Jabo stood watching her as she disappeared, holding a handful of her hair.

❧

My great-grandmother ended the story there by saying, "And honey, ever since that day, the eagle has had a bald head. So be yourself and be thankful." She later mentioned that, after this, whenever Jabo met a woman, the first thing he did was ask to see her feet.

Many years later I read another version of this story, which Mary Alicia Owen had collected in St. Joseph, Missouri, in the 1870s or 1880s. I wondered if my great-grandfather first heard the story in Missouri. Unlike my great-grandmother, my great-grandfather wasn't religious and didn't tell us stories to discipline us. His stories were very entertaining, but in the process of being entertained I learned many lessons from the man who, I believed, knew all there was to know about everything. My great-grandfather's name was Pete Cofer, and we called him Uncle Pete. Everyone who knew him called him Uncle Pete, except my mother—she called him Granddaddy, perhaps because he told such grand stories. I would listen to him in wide-eyed wonder expecting him, at any given moment, to spread hidden wings and take angelic flight.

"He ain't nothin' but the devil," my great-grandmother said, after she kicked him out of the house because of his drinking. I was more than a little upset. I wanted to run away from home. Although my great-grandfather talked me out of that notion, even he couldn't stop me from sneaking over to the boardinghouse where he lived. I just had to see him and hear him tell me a story. His gestures were as mesmerizing as the changes in his voice as he told about "The Man in the Moon" or "The Talkin' Dog," the "Cotton Pickin' Cotton" or "The Sun and the Moon," "Uncle Son and Mule Men" or other mysterious characters lurking in the plots of his repertoire of stories. He could be funny, he could be sad. His face became a rubber canvas of action as he growled like a bear, howled like the old north wind, barked like a dog, or mimicked my great-grandmother. He could become a horse, a drum, a stubborn mule, a clucking hen, or a kind young girl. I could hear them all. I could see them all—right there as

Uncle Pete told me his stories, transporting me to another time or another place.

Some of his stories were true, I am sure, but some of them were so outlandish—I had to wonder when he told us stories like "The Sun and the Moon."

Uncle Pete told us that if we didn't fight we'd be okay. But if we fought other children and made trouble with other people, we'd be just like the moon. Uncle Pete swore that the sun and the moon used to live in the sky together in the daytime. But everyone praised the sun, told the sun how wonderful and bright it was, how the sun's shine and the warm rays were so welcome.

"Well," he said, "the moon got just a little bit jealous. So the moon decided that it would go around to the trees and go around to the plants and to the animals, and anyone else who would listen, and talk about the sun. And the moon tiptoed around and told the trees, 'Pssst, pssst, pssst, pssst.' It was so bad, I can't repeat it," Uncle Pete said. "Well, as gossip usually does, eventually this gossip got back to the sun.

"Well, the sun was hot." That's what Uncle Pete said. He said, "You know that sun got *hot*!" He stamped his foot. Uncle Pete was very expressive when he told the story.

He said, "And when the sun gets hot, honey, you better *watch out*! Watch out!

"Well, when the sun heard what the moon said, the sun went over there." Uncle Pete stomps across the floor swinging his hips (and you know by that walk that the sun is a woman). "So the sun went over to the moon," and raising her voice, "'Did you say pssst, pssst, pssst, pssst?' The moon said," dropping its voice, "'Oh no! Oh, no!' So the sun said, 'I better not find out you did!' And the sun walked away again."

Uncle Pete stomps across the floor, swinging his hips.

"And people started praising the sun. And this time, the moon said to itself, 'I don't care if she does find out. I'm gonna go and talk some more. Pssst, pssst, pssst, pssst, and psssssssst!' Really nasty stuff this time.

"Well, I guess the moon expected this to happen. And whether the moon expected it or not, the gossip got back to the sun."

And Uncle Pete said, "Ooooh, this time the sun was *really hot*! I mean *really hot*!" (We were tempted to ask if the sun had ever been cold, but we didn't do that.)

"So this time the sun went over to the moon, no questions asked. Bam, bam, bam, bam! And beat up the moon really bad."

Well, the moon was so embarrassed that it slunk on out. Uncle Pete said, "That moon just snuck away. Just snuck on outa there like a slinky skunk."

So we said, "Well, Uncle Pete, what happened to the moon?"

And then he said, "Well," he said, "the moon was beat up so bad, and was so embarrassed, that the first time it came back out, the first time it could ever show its face, it just snuck on in at night and showed about a quarter of its face. And a little while later it snuck on in at night again, and showed about half of its face. And a little while later, the moon got brave and showed off *all* its face. But chil'ren, you know to this day, the moon only shows its face once in a while. So don't you go gossipin' about nobody, or you won't be able to show your face all the time."

Uncle Pete often boasted about the Indian and African blood that flowed through his veins. I was proud to know of that and dreamed of one day visiting Africa. He never delved deeply into his heritage. He just wanted the world and anybody in the world who would listen to know that he knew who and what he was. He walked the streets of our town in New Jersey, long silky black hair flying in the breeze, a whip in his hand and with an air that meant "Don't mess with me." And no one ever did. He was kind and patient with me, but my mom argued for many years that he loved her best.

Since becoming an adult and a professional storyteller, and especially since I began working with other storytellers, I have reflected quite a bit on my great-grandfather's tales. Some of them have become the impetus for my research and the inspiration for stories I share with my husband, Truman, our children, grandchildren, and audiences throughout Missouri.

I met my husband Truman in July 1971 in Scranton, Pennsylvania, where I was working. Our different paths had taken us to the same

Gladys and Truman Coggswell on their Pennsylvania farm, where they shared family stories during the long winters and dreamed of moving west. (Coggswell Collection)

places a number of times before we met, and we often wonder if this was coincidence or providence. We were married at the Methodist Parsonage in Equinunk, Pennsylvania, on February 12, 1972.

Truman had a forty-acre farm in Lookout, Pennsylvania, and during the long winter evenings he told me all about his life and his family in New England. He was born in Bridgeport, Connecticut, on October 16, 1934, and he had many interesting stories about his boyhood and his family heritage. He has a twin brother and three sisters, all of the Narragansett Indian Reservation in Westerly, Rhode Island.

"My father, Theodore William Coggswell, Sr.—'The Paheia,' or 'Little Pony'—was born in New Milford, Connecticut, on August 15, 1905, and was raised there," Truman said. "His father, William Truman Coggswell, born on April 22, 1867, in Kent, Connecticut, was raised on the Schaghticoke Indian Reservation about fifteen miles

Truman Coggswell's grandfather William Truman Coggswell, High Sachem, Schaghticoke Tribe of Native Americans, who have a long history in the Housatonic River valley of Connecticut. (Courtesy Truman Coggswell)

north of New Milford. It was from this grandfather that I have my first name, Truman.

"My middle name, Hill, comes from my maternal grandfather, whose name was William Berry Hill. He was from Bridgeport. Both my paternal and maternal grandfathers were great sportsmen and belonged to the same hunting club. Together, around the turn of the century, they often went big game hunting in Canada."

Truman's family name was originally the Pootatuck Indian name Co'shuree, which is related to the name Cockshure, one of the chiefs who signed deeds conveying the land to the English in 1733. The presence of the Co'shuree, Cogswell, or Coggswell family in the area is documented in Connecticut historical records of Native Americans dating from 1639. Truman is listed with the Bureau of Indian Affairs in Washington, D.C., as a Schaghticoke Indian, a descendant of the historical tribe. The name Schaghticoke is pronounced "P'ska'ti'kuk."

Truman told me that his mother, Mary Francis Hill-Coggswell, was born on March 28, 1915, in Bridgeport, Connecticut. Her mother, Lillian Amanda Banks-Hill, had been born in New Orleans, Louisiana, on October 17, 1880, of Choctaw/Coushatta Indian and African American descent. His grandmother spent her school years in Mobile, Alabama, but shortly after she graduated from one of Mobile's high schools, her father moved the family to Nashville, Tennessee. She graduated from Fisk University in the class of 1900 and was married to William B. Hill on June 24 of that year, in a wedding that was covered by Nashville newspapers. It was one of the largest social events of the time. William Hill was from Bridgeport, Connecticut, and after their marriage Truman's grandparents made their home in Bridgeport. His grandmother attended Yale University and afterward taught in the Americanization program in Bridgeport for thirty-four years, before she retired at age seventy-five. On her ninety-second birthday she was honored by Fisk University as the school's oldest living graduate. Throughout her life she was active in many civic causes, including the Women's Suffrage Movement.

Truman recalled how he spent his summer months with his grandparents and other of his father's kin at New Milford and on the Schaghticoke Indian Reservation.

∾

During these summer months, our grandparents and other elders gathered us around to tell us of many things in the world and their meanings. They told us of our Native American ancestors. We learned about the ceremonial songs and dances giving thanks and showing respect for the life-giving force. They taught us what our ancestors taught them: that it was important not to upset the natural order of things but, instead, sustain a natural balance of nature's life-giving forces, which would ensure our people's survival.

Our parents emphasized that we should listen to the older people, so we would learn our history and traditions, and at a very early age we often asked our grandmother, who was responsible for not letting us wander too far off, when she was going to tell the story of the Mukeeweesuag People. She would always reply, "Very soon, I will tell you that story!" When we reached the proper age to hear it, she told us the story of the Mukeeweesuag People, who are the little people "about so high," she said. We would know them by their strange manners and dress. They lived deep in the woods and along the riverbanks and "If you go there you will surely see them," she said, "and they will point their fingers at you, and you will go blind. Then they will carry you off where you will never be seen again."

When we were old enough to go off and play by ourselves, she told us the story of "Old Granny Schreechchum," who lived on a small island in the middle of the big river, which was always surrounded by a thick fog, so that at times only the tops of the trees could be seen. She warned us that if we wandered too close to the big river's banks we would certainly hear her eerie screams and screeches. If that happened, she said, "You will lose your balance and fall into the big river, and the swift rapids of the river will carry you away."

∿

Truman told me that during his early school years his teachers in Bridgeport noticed he liked to draw. "My grandmother, Mama Hill, and my teachers always encouraged me in my artwork," he said, "and during this time I decided to be an artist when I grew up. At Warren High School in Bridgeport, my classmates voted me the class artist for our yearbook, and I won first place in a Brotherhood Poster Art Contest in a competition with other area high schools."

Truman remembers with pride the day he received the first place award for the Brotherhood Poster. First Lady Eleanor Roosevelt was there and presented it to him. Dr. Ralph J. Bunch— the first black non-diplomatic official in the U.S. State Department—also attended the presentation. Dr. Bunch had transferred to the United Nations in 1947, and as the highest-ranking American in the United

Like many eastern emigrants before them, Gladys and Truman moved to Missouri in 1974, settling first in Doniphan and then in St. Louis, where Gladys attended the University of St. Louis at Forest Park and Truman found work as the senior illustrator in the Electronic and Space Division of Emerson Electric Company. (Coggswell Collection)

Nations, he had mediated the end of the Arab-Israeli War in 1949. In 1950 Dr. Bunch became the first black American to win the Nobel Peace Prize. Meeting Dr. Bunch and Mrs. Roosevelt made a deep impression on Truman. He knew Mrs. Roosevelt had made it possible for Marian Anderson to sing for thousands of people in front of the Lincoln Memorial on Easter Sunday, 1939, when the Daughters of the American Revolution denied her the right to sing in Constitution Hall.

After graduating from high school in 1952, Truman joined the U.S. Marine Corps to fulfill his military obligation and served three years of active duty during the Korean War. After honorable discharge from the Marine Corps, he moved to New York City to pursue a career in commercial art and illustration. During those early years in New York, Truman took college courses in commercial art and evening painting classes at the Art Students League of New York City, supporting himself by working for advertising agencies. Later he and his brother developed a business in New Jersey to work with Original Equipment Manufacturers. After he moved to Pennsylvania, he developed his farm and served commercial art clients in New Jersey, New York, and Pennsylvania, which led to our meeting in Scranton in 1971. After we moved to Missouri in 1974, Truman continued working in the field of commercial illustration and taught photographic and dye transfer retouching at Forest Park Community College in St. Louis. He officially retired from this work in 1998 after forty-two years in the field.

During our years in Pennsylvania, Truman and I had the opportunity to visit my family in New Jersey and also to visit Truman's family and the Schaghticoke Indian Reservation in Connecticut. We heard more stories from both families. After we migrated to Missouri, following in the footsteps of many earlier migrants to the Midwest, we continued telling stories, and in 1992, before Truman retired, we started a storytelling organization in Missouri called "By Word of Mouth Storytelling Guild." The annual storytelling conference and festival drew storytellers from throughout Missouri and Illinois each year. We have continued storytelling, always exchanging stories with others.

This book includes some of the stories that family and community storytellers—or griots—living in Missouri have shared with us. As folklorist Dana Everts-Boehm explained in the 1982 publication "A Handful of Dinky," in which she discussed African American storytelling in Missouri, the "griot," or community storyteller in West Africa, is a "highly trained professional who chronicles tribal history and genealogy, and is also trained in oral history, music, and traditional narration." In the United States and in Missouri, "the term is used more loosely as a designation for African American storytellers and oral historians." Although "these individuals have not undergone the same kind of rigorous training as their African counterparts," as Everts-Boehm wrote, nevertheless, family and community storytellers are handing down stories of "the way it was" (in Mr. Jerry Grimmett's words) and preserving an important part of Missouri's African American heritage.

The cultural life of Missouri's African Americans during the last half of the twentieth century remains largely untold in the state's recorded history. The rich oral tradition that has sustained families and communities is largely unknown to the younger generation. By sharing their stories and experiences, family and community story-tellers have contributed immeasurably to my own knowledge. We believe making the stories available will enrich the lives of both black and white residents in their communities and throughout the state.

# 1

# Finding Frankford

Truman and I now live in Frankford, a small town in Pike County, Missouri. When people ask me how I came to be in Missouri, I almost always say, "It was divine intervention." We did not plan to move here, but, tired of being snowed in on our hilltop in Pennsylvania every winter, we decided to sell our farm in Equinunk. The buyer wanted to move his family in before Christmas, so during the second week of December 1974 we packed our belongings in a U-Haul truck, hitched it to our station wagon, and headed west—destination, we thought, Minnesota. We ran into a heavy snowstorm in Columbus, Ohio, and had to get off the highway and stay overnight there. The next day we decided to change our plans and drive south. To this day I cannot explain why we ended up in Missouri, but several days before Christmas, we bought a house in Doniphan, Missouri.

Some years later we learned that we had been the talk of the area because we were the first non-whites to move there since the Civil War. Our stay in the Ozarks did not last long. Since no work was available in the Doniphan area, we lived there only about eight months before deciding to buy a house and move to University City, a small suburb of St. Louis. Hoping to find a small farm, we drove up through northeast Missouri almost every weekend from spring through fall. After years of searching, we bought several acres of land with no dwelling that we used for weekend camping.

One Saturday, while driving south on Highway 61 from Hannibal, the sign to Frankford beckoned us. For no apparent reason, as if hypnotized, we drove into the town and parked on Main Street, in front of the Daisy Patch Art and Craft Center. I stepped out of the car, and as my foot touched the ground I felt something I had never experienced before and have not felt since. It was a surge of emotion that made me feel I had been here before and this was where I belonged. I had never before in my life felt that I belonged anywhere. Influenced by the power of fate and circumstance, with no planning and not much discussion, we quickly bought a little place and moved to Frankford. This was in the spring of 1981, less than a month after our initial visit. We have never regretted our move.

Long before setting foot on Missouri soil, however, I had heard about the state from Uncle Pete, who claimed to have Missouri roots. I have often wondered if he knew of Frankford or perhaps may have even passed through our unique little town in his wanderings. I have found a family of Cofers in St. Louis. Two of them have owned African American bookstores. In 1993 Andre Cofer was a vendor at our first By Word of Mouth Storytelling Guild Conference and Festival in Hannibal. I would be as proud to be related to these Missouri Cofers as I am proud to be related to my great-grandfather Cofer. I know Uncle Pete Cofer's spirit is with me, especially when I am telling a story, and I just let him take over.

Both Truman and I are storytellers by nature, and like the early settlers in Missouri we brought our stories west with us to share with our neighbors. We soon found stories in abundance in our new hometown. We learned that the town of Frankford, in Peno township, was first laid out in 1819 on land owned by Solomon Fisher. Samuel Redding had come from Kentucky three years before, in 1816, and spent the first winter in a cave a few miles northeast of what was to become the town. The next year Lawrence Killebrew, a Methodist minister and a root and herb doctor, came from St. Charles County, "prepared to take care of both the spiritual and physical health of the area residents," as Frankford historian Mrs. J. H. Lowry wrote.

In 1856 Elizabeth Fisher sold a corner lot on what is now King Street to "Garrison, Sr., a colored man," and the town became incorporated three years later. In 1865 "Garrison Gardener, a free colored man, and Nancy Gardener sold the property to Pleasant Randolph, a free colored man," who held it until 1892. Several owners later, in July 1981, Truman and I bought the property at 419 King Street and have felt very much at home there. From Mrs. Lowry, who wrote an account of early life in Frankford in 1905, we learned that the first shoemaker in town was "old uncle Garrison Gardener, a black man," who worked "day and night over his shoe bench." At that time customers furnished the leather for their shoes, and some of them "would frighten a horse to death," according to Mrs. Lowry. Another craft "carried on principally by the old colored people" was creating split baskets, from the "smallest size to the largest," but by 1905 basketmaking was a "lost art." Black residents also made "all kinds of candles, bread trays, rolling pins, and other useful articles" in nineteenth-century Frankford.

A tradition still treasured in Frankford, which we soon learned about, is Choir Day.

> By and by, when the morning comes
> When all the saints are gone to gather home
> We're gonna tell the story of how we overcome
> And we'll understand it better by and by.

Anyone who has ever attended an African American church service in the last hundred years is familiar with this old gospel tune. It is just one of the many moving gospel songs you might hear on Choir Day, an annual celebration hosted by various African American churches in northeast Missouri. Frankford's annual Choir Day is held the first Sunday in May at the Frankford Bethel African Methodist Episcopal Church.

According to the latest census, Frankford now has a residential population of 351. Seven are African American. On Choir Day, however, when African Americans "Gather Home" to celebrate the living, the dead, and those yet to be born, the African American

The Coggswells moved to Frankford in Pike County in 1982 and found a small but welcoming African American community. Choir Day is a long-established tradition in Frankford, and in 1953 the Frankford Choir, including Mrs. Marie Campbell, her son Bill Campbell, Mrs. Camie Doolin, and others performed in Bowling Green. (Coggswell Collection)

visitors outnumber the population of the entire town. Around eleven o'clock in the morning, a carry-in meal is served buffet style. There is always more than enough good food, tea, coffee, and water.

At one o'clock the Choir Day Celebration begins with a prayer, congregational singing, testifying, recognition of visiting ministers, and a memorial for those who crossed on over to the other side during the year. Announcements are made so that everyone will know where and when the remaining churches will host their Choir Day. A representative from each choir signs in as the group arrives, and the list is given to the Mistress of Ceremonies—most likely the Reverend Faye Vaughn. Then the battle of the choirs is on. All are warmly welcomed as they march in with a song, followed by two more soul-stirring selections. It is not unusual for as many as forty choirs to participate on Choir Day in Frankford. There is never enough room

Mrs. Marie Campbell has made preserving Frankford's African American heritage her cause for many years. She shared with the newcomers many stories concerning the history of the community. (Courtesy Mrs. Campbell)

inside the church, which means that many of the choirs must wait outside before marching in to sing.

It will most likely be after five o'clock when people finally file out of the church and head back downstairs (which has a separate entrance) to retrieve their mostly empty carry-in pie plates, cake carriers, casserole dishes, pots and pans. Folks exchange parting words, hugs, kisses, and waves and then head for their cars. Once local and visiting volunteers finish the cleaning up, the church doors are locked, and the church stands quietly empty until the first Sunday in May rolls around again. Around April 1 of the following year, Mrs. Marie Campbell will send out invitations to about thirty churches, asking that the church choir prepare to sing an "A and B" selection for the next Choir Day. Everyone who comes, whether to sing or to listen, is expected to bring a covered dish, and all bring something to share.

Mrs. Campbell, the former Marie King of New London, moved to Frankford in 1944 as the bride of Frankford native Raymond Campbell, who died on June 6, 1987, at the age of sixty-four. Their son,

William "Bill" Campbell, owns an insurance company in St. Louis, but he makes time to visit and sing with the choir on Choir Day. According to Mrs. Campbell, Frankford's Choir Day Celebration is about fifty-five years old. When I first interviewed her in 2001, she recalled the many changes that have taken place in the Frankford community since she came.

∼

Frankford had a choir that was started by my sister-in-law, Leona Campbell—we called her "Sis." They all left. Some died, some moved, but most of the ones who moved came back for Choir Day. Their children, grandchildren, nieces, nephews, other relatives, and friends came too. You know there were once enough blacks in and around Frankford to support two churches, a masonic hall, and a cemetery. There was always something going on. The upkeep of the buildings and cemetery was paid for with proceeds from our rallies, renting out the church for school closing activities, personal donations, and entertainment. It seems that there was never a shortage of help.

At one time Frankford only had one cemetery. Blacks were buried on one side and whites on the other. Then the highway (Route C) came through and divided the land. There was improved cemetery on one side and unimproved pasture on another. Somehow the pasture became the black cemetery, and black men worked really hard to improve that piece of land. They didn't have any weed eaters, lawn mowers, or modern equipment. They sawed trees and worked the pasture by hand. I can still remember helping with meals and taking them to the cemetery to feed the men who were working there. I am seventy-seven years old and I've seen a lot of changes—some good and some bad, but no one could have made me believe that our country would be attacked the way it was. My late husband was a soldier, my son retired after twenty years in the service, and one of my grandsons is in the service now, so I understand about war and duty, but I don't understand this. I hope it all gets straightened out and that the world will know peace.

～

During the spring, summer, and early fall, Mrs. Campbell can be seen on her riding mower, taking care of the grounds of the church, masonic hall, and the cemetery. She has almost single-handedly maintained all of the African American sites in Frankford, but she admits that even she is slowing down a little now. On her seventy-seventh birthday, in 2001, her friends and family gave her a surprise birthday party. Banners were hung in various places about town, and she was led to believe she was attending a church service at First Christian Church, where the party was held. She was both surprised and pleased at the recognition the community showed for her contributions to Frankford.

Other valued African American members of the Frankford community are the Reverend Faye Vaughn and Mr. Robert "Bobby Gene" Vaughn, who have been married for fifty-three years. Rev. Vaughn shared some of her memories of becoming a part of the Frankford community as a newcomer. When she first married Bob, a lifelong resident of the community who had been born in his grandmother's house in Frankford, everybody wanted to know about her. She remembers they welcomed her with open arms, engaging her in conversation, telling her about Bob and his childhood, and asking questions about her.

～

There were crank phones then, and party lines. We didn't have a phone at first, so we relied on messages from Aunt Camie Doolin and her husband, Uncle Elmer. Gradually we got private phones.

I remember a man that I thought everybody called "Paul," so I called him "Mister Paul." One day I was talking to Bob about him and he let me know that they were calling him "Pa," not Paul.

The Reverend Burton was the preacher for the Second

Christian Church. He came once a month. He lived in Madison, Missouri, and was known as a circuit preacher. He preached here for forty years. The Methodist preacher also came once a month, but on a different Sunday from Rev. Burton. People went to both churches, and Mrs. Camie Doolin played the piano for both churches. So we weren't sure what denomination anybody was, because they all went to whatever church had a preacher. You didn't know if they were Christian or Methodist or in-between. The same principle applied to the choir—it was neither Christian Church nor Methodist, but for everybody who could sing.

Bob's mother and sister-in-law were the founders of the Frankford Community Choir. His mother, Mrs. Hawkins, was an accomplished piano player. It amazes me how much they could do with so very little. When I came to Frankford, Aunt Camie and Miss Ola were matriarchs of the churches. Miss Ola was the matriarch of the Methodist Church and Aunt Camie the matriarch of the Christian Church. They all cooperated. They would have a fish fry and make two or three hundred dollars together. That was fifty-three years ago.

In New London, where I pastor, if we clear two or three hundred dollars for a fish fry or a chicken dinner we are doing well—we should be making a thousand dollars! So we're not having fish fries and chicken dinners anymore. Now we just let people donate the amount they were going to give. They just put the donation in a jar. In two or three months' time, we have five hundred dollars or more, and we didn't have to work Saturdays at all. Nobody's talking about who didn't buy any food or who went shopping and left others to clean up the dirty kitchen. We just talk about how happy we are.

One of the strange things in Frankford is the evergreen tree by the Christian Church. It was only a couple of years old when I first came here, just a little bitty thing. Now it is very big, very tall. I paid attention to that. People in Frankford used to go to the springs to get water. Now they can no longer get water from the springs because they have been cemented.

Bob says farmers used to come to Frankford and would go to the spring and water their horses. He remembers when they had hitching posts downtown. Farmers came to town with their horses and wagons. I thought that was just in Wild West movies. We used to have a doctor, a barbershop, and a grocery store. All those people came to Frankford, and now they are gone. Louis Cox was in St. Louis when I came, but his mother and father were here. He had a filling station and a garage in St. Louis, but when his wife died he moved back here. That was about thirty years ago.

Virginia Unsell, a white woman, was a very good teacher. When integration started in Frankford about 1960 there was no kindergarten. Children started school in the first grade. Mrs. Unsell was the only teacher who told me that my son Bud had trouble with his eyes. My son Curtis, who is studying to be a physician's assistant, told me that he wishes she was still alive to see him become a physician's assistant. She was so nice.

～

The Reverend Vaughn says she grew up in Bowling Green and lived there for eighteen years. "When I go back and visit the black cemetery," she says, "I realize how many people I've known in my lifetime. Most of my childhood memories are now in that cemetery."

I told Rev. Vaughn that, when we moved to Frankford, Mrs. Unsell sold us the house we live in and I miss her too.

The value placed on education by the black community is a major theme in many of the stories told to me by the residents of Frankford and others in northeast Missouri. One of the stories Mrs. Camie Doolin told me to demonstrate the importance of being on time is a good example. I later told her story to a young audience in Jefferson City, and I may have exaggerated a little when I described Mrs. Camie. In fact, if my grandmother had heard me she may have said I was fibbing, but the story is just as Mrs. Camie told it.

When we moved to Frankford, I told the children, I met a very interesting woman. Her name was Mrs. Camie Doolin. And I think

Mrs. Doolin was every bit of two hundred years old. And she had the most wonderful stories, but she was also very stern with everyone. And I remember her inviting us to her church. And we were a little bit late. And she said to us, "Now you all better try to start bein' on time, or you gonna find yourself holdin' a handful of Dinky."

Well I didn't know what that meant. And I found it odd that she would say such a thing in church. And she noticed that I was looking puzzled, so she said, "Oh, ho, ho. You don't know about the handful a-Dinky, do you?" And, of course, I didn't. So she went on to explain to me.

~

Long ago in Frankford, the African American children could not go to the high school because the high school was only for white children. And so they would have to go to Hannibal to go to high school. And we went in this little caboose—at that time we had a railroad track in Frankford and a train, which we don't have any more. We went in this little caboose, which they called the Dinky.

Well, there was this young man, Raymond Campbell, who was always late. And the person who drove the caboose would always wait for him—the conductor would always wait for Raymond. Well, he got tired of waiting for Raymond. Everybody got tired of waiting for Raymond. And you know how young people are sometimes. And they said, "Leave him! Leave him! Just leave him!" Well, the conductor listened to them and they started to leave.

Well, here comes Raymond, just a runnin' down the track, just a runnin' and Raymond caught up with that Dinky and grabbed a handful of Dinky and held on.

~

And that is why Mrs. Camie Doolin was talking about a handful of Dinky. Because Raymond had to hold on to that Dinky all the way to Hannibal. One of the lessons in Mrs. Doolin's story was "Don't be late," but the underlying theme is that education was so important

African American students in Frankford attended high school in Hannibal, some riding a train called "The Dinky," and former students attended a high school reunion in Hannibal before Douglass School closed. Robert Vaughn is third from the left. (Coggswell Collection, courtesy Robert Vaughn)

to this young man that he held on to the Dinky all the way from Frankford to Hannibal, about thirty miles, so he could be in school that day.

From Mrs. Doolin, who died in the early 1980s at only ninety-nine, I also learned local stories about "patterollers" (white patrollers who looked for runaways during slavery days), about black midwives, clever mules, and African American schools. One of the stories Mrs. Doolin told me was about a runaway slave—her grandfather. He knew he had to have a pass to go from one place to another, but he didn't have a pass. He couldn't read or write, but he could make marks that looked like letters, and he thought, "Those patterollers ain't no more smarter than me." So he wrote something down, that was not his name, not his pass, not written by his owner. He showed it to the patrollers and they let him pass because they could not read either. As Mrs. Doolin said, "He just walked right on to Freedom and never stopped!"

Gravestones of former Union soldiers in "Little Africa" cemetery near Louisiana, Pike County, Missouri. (Dana Everts-Boehm photo; courtesy Missouri Folk Arts Program)

Near the town of Louisiana in Pike County, Missouri, is the site of "Little Africa," and local oral historians, including Mrs. Doolin, Mr. Leroy Berry, and Mrs. Vivian Smith remembered that Little Africa once belonged to the largest slaveholder in the region, Malcolm Redding, owner of the Redding Brick Company. Much of the area was wooded, and it served as a hideout for runaway slaves before the Civil War. According to local legend, Little Africa had an African American community of runaway slaves before emancipation. According to Frankford resident Hardy Wilson, Redding, a white farmer, gave forty acres to each of his ex-slaves after the Civil War, and these plots, joined together, became a post–Civil War rural black settlement.

One of the few indications that a black community once developed in Little Africa is an overgrown cemetery. Two tombstones remain, those of two men who had joined two of the seven black regiments raised in Missouri during the Civil War to fight for the Union. Dana

Everts-Boehm reported that 3,700 black recruits had enlisted in Missouri's Colored Infantry by February 1864. Of these, 356 were from Louisiana in Pike County, near Little Africa. According to Antonio Holland, a total number of about 8,000 black recruits from Missouri joined the Union Army in 1863 and 1864. Among them were some of the soldiers who, toward the end of the war, raised funds to establish Lincoln Institute, now Lincoln University, to train black teachers. In Pike County, as elsewhere, former slaves longed to see their children have the opportunity to get schooling, to learn to read and write.

# 2

# Getting to Know Hannibal

The contributions and cultural experiences of the African American community in the area were not often included by historians in written narratives and books relating to the history of Hannibal, Missouri. The Mississippi River town in Marion County is located, according to geographer Robert M. Crisler, on the edge of the region known as "Little Dixie." Some historians describe the Little Dixie region as beginning in Callaway and other counties north of the Missouri River in central Missouri and reaching westward to Lafayette, Saline, and Clay counties, but Crisler also includes Ralls, a county lying between Pike and Marion, as one of the Little Dixie counties. He considers Pike and Marion as "periphery or outer" counties in the region. When Hannibal emerged as a destination for tourism in the late 1940s, the central historical symbol in local tourism sites, and until recently public memorials, centered on the life of Samuel Clemens, otherwise known as Mark Twain, who lived in Hannibal as a boy.

A vital, but once hidden, history lives on, however, in the hearts and minds of African American residents, continuing through their oral narratives and remembrances. Conducting a research project focused on African American cultural traditions and oral narratives in Missouri, I interviewed a number of African Americans in Hannibal,

The late Mrs. Dorine Ambers shared her memories of childhood experiences in the Hannibal area and told of her work with the National Association of Colored Women's Clubs. (Coggswell Collection)

in their homes and at family or school reunions, cultural festivals, and other traditional gatherings. These interviews produced an abundance of narratives revealing a rich culture, stories of establishing institutions, art and civic organizations, local businesses, and community support systems that not only survived but thrived in spite of the challenges inherent in the so-called separate but equal system of segregation. Their life stories and traditional narratives reveal how the African American visionaries of Hannibal launched local businesses and created cultural organizations, utilizing their entrepreneurial skills to better their lives and advance themselves, their families, and community members both before and during the struggle for integration.

Mrs. Minnie Dorine Chester Ambers is one inspiring example. She was born in Withers Mill, Missouri, but her family moved to Hannibal when she was six years old. She became a dedicated clubwoman, a master cook, and an extraordinary storyteller. Most of Mrs. Ambers's stories of her experiences were the kind that motivated me to head for the library to see if I could find additional information. It was through her that I first became aware of the existence of the National Association of Colored Women's Clubs (NACWC).

I learned from her that the first NACWC conference was held in Boston, on July 29–31, 1895. Five years later, in 1900, the Missouri Association of Colored Women's Clubs (MACWC) was organized. Seven clubs formed the nucleus of the state organization, three of which were based in St. Louis: Harpers, the Wednesday Afternoon Service Club, and the Orphan's Home Association. The other clubs were based in Columbia, Jefferson City, Kansas City, and St. Joseph. Mrs. Susan Vashon was the first state president of MACWC. Josephine Silone Yates, another famous Missouri name I had not heard until I interviewed Mrs. Ambers, was a teacher at Lincoln University in Jefferson City who served as national president of the organization. In 1904, during Yates's presidency, St. Louis hosted the national convention.

On July 26, 1904, under the leadership of Mrs. Yates, the MACWC was granted incorporation status in the state of Missouri by the City of St. Louis Circuit Court. Certification was filed, and a copy was issued on August 2, 1904. There are now approximately a thousand NACWC clubs nationwide, and members include women from all walks of life. The overall motto is "Lifting as We Climb." Mrs. Ambers's life's work was grounded in honoring that motto. In 1962 she joined the Monday Art Club in Quincy, Illinois, because Hannibal did not have an organization for arts that was open to African American women. In 1971 she became a charter member and first president of the Fannie Griffin Art Club (FGAC) of Hannibal. Fannie Griffin is a retired nurse, who continues to carry on the civic and art-related duties of the club that bears her name. The FGAC immediately became an affiliate of the MACWC. It was the first group in Hannibal to offer scholarships to African American students in Hannibal who wanted a college education. Mrs. Ambers recalls that the first scholarship awarded was to Estralita Jones, who is now a scientist. Estralita's mother continues to live in Hannibal and to work with the art club.

In 1983 Mrs. Ambers, then Mrs. Dorine Chester, was elected president of the Illinois Association of Colored Women's Clubs. In 1987 she was elected president of the MACWC. Shortly after the Missouri election, at the age of sixty-nine, she married her childhood sweetheart, Roscoe William Ambers. She never gave up her membership in the Illinois Association of Colored Women's Clubs in Quincy, and she is the only woman in the history of the NACWC to have served as president of two state chapters of the organization. She was also recognized for her outstanding leadership as the NACWC's National Sickle Cell Chairperson. Mrs. Ambers held many jobs as a cook and was best known for her "magic touch" in making pie crusts and blackberry cobblers. Of her jobs, she said, "The hours were always too long and the pay was always too short." She and her best friend, Lola Richardson, worked as cooks at the Hannibal Country Club for many years. She explained,

~

Blacks could cook for white members of the club, but we couldn't eat there. I think it was in the early sixties when the first black person was a guest there. It was during a high school graduation party. The white kids insisted on bringing their black friend and they seemed to have a ball. I know that some of the grownups didn't like it. The boy's name was Larry Thompson.

~

Mrs. Ambers would have laughed out loud from pure joy if she had been there on May 10, 2001, when that same Larry Thompson was appointed to the position of Deputy Attorney General to the United States, his appointment approved by 19 yeas and 0 nays.

Dorine Ambers passed away on September 2, 2000, at the age of eighty-one. The Fifty Year Douglass School Reunion Souvenir Journal of 1992 has a quote that exemplifies her life.

A chapter completed,
a page turned,
a life well lived,
a rest well earned.

One of the stories Mrs. Ambers told me was of one of her earliest memories.

∽

In Withers Mill, we lived behind a little farm next door to the great big farm owned by some white people. [The owner] told grandpa to take the children in the house and keep them in the house because they were going to have a rally. Well, I was nosy. They put us into the house early. We didn't get to go outdoors and play, we were supposedly going back to bed, but I waited until everybody went to sleep and crept out and went out in the yard and saw all these people. I thought they were ghosts, they scared me so bad I couldn't cry and I couldn't holler or nothing because I wasn't supposed to be out there. . . . Looked like they had on white sheets and hats and stuff and I was scared to death. I went in and woke up my sister Jane and told her to come and see what I was looking at. We checked back out and scared her to death, we couldn't even holler 'cause grandpa and grandma told us don't go out there meddling outdoors. I tell you we was scared all night long, we didn't go to sleep. We were so scared that these ghosts were going to get us. Of course we learned later on thru the years that it was a Ku Klux Klan rally. The man next door was a grand dragon I guess. That's what it was, the Klan. And you know he was just as kind as he could be to grandpa and grandma and us.

One time after we moved to Hannibal we lived down kind of like in the bottoms and there was a big hill way over from, I would say, several blocks from us, and one night I looked up and there was somethin' burning. And we hollered for Mom. "Come here," we said, "they are burning up the hill or something." And she come running to see what we seen. And they were burning that cross up there. . . . We didn't know what it was. She said, "That is the Ku Klux Klan burning a cross. It's to frighten people." And then we said, "What's Klan? What they look like?" And she proceeded to tell us, but we already . . . seen them. That's when we knew what the Ku Klux Klan was.

∽

As a small child, Dorine Ambers slipped out of the house one evening and saw a scene that would puzzle her for many years. (From an anti Ku Klux Klan pamphlet in the Hyde Papers, 1921–1924, University of Missouri Western Historical Manuscript Collection, Columbia)

Mrs. Ambers liked to tell me a story that I was already familiar with, but her voice, gestures, and laughter made the story sound brand new. "I'd Be just like Old Mose," she would say, and we would enjoy the story together again.

～

I'd be just like Old Mose. You know he was a slave, but first chance he got, he used the Underground Railroad and quick turned his back on slavery. Got as far as Missouri—trying to get to Illinois because it was a free state. Ain't that something? Well, he musta missed his connection because he was stuck there for a few days. So he would hide out, and every now and then, when he thought it was safe, he'd do some begging. One day he saw a white man and asked him for a dime. Said he wanted to get something to eat.

White man asked him if he was a runaway.

He answered, "Yes sah."

White man asked him didn't he get plenty of food where he was a slave.

"Yes sah."

White man asked, "Well, why in the devil would you wanna run away?"

"Because I'm supposed to be free, sah."

White man said, "I won't give you one cent. You better go back where you can get a plenty to eat and don't have to beg. Slavery sounds like a good job to me."

"Lemme tell you somethin' 'bout that job," Mose said. "Hit's still open, and I ain't goin' back to it, but you is welcome to go try it for your own since you think it's such a good thing. Thank you very much."

～

Many historians have observed that "scholarly literature on the African American neighborhood and community development in the Jim Crow era is slim." Stories of everyday life, institutional formation, leisure activities, and other workings of society—whether from a historical, sociological, geographical, or anthropological framework—have taken a back seat to civil rights era narratives and school desegregation experiences. Stories collected in Hannibal and other Missouri towns demonstrate that memories of pre-integration African American cultural and social life still linger.

Mrs. Lillian Jones has lived in Hannibal all of her life. One of thirteen children, she has been a member of Willow Street Christian Church since infancy. She was baptized in a creek. A 1946 graduate of Douglass School in Hannibal, Mrs. Jones said there was a wide choice of studies to prepare the students for the world. She listed Latin, Spanish, French, Music Appreciation, Nurse Training, Cooking, Sewing, and Athletics in addition to the usual basic subjects. Like many African Americans, she recalls her dismay on hearing that the Douglass School would be closed forever. In the summer of 1954, former and current students were so sorry to hear that old Douglass was closing her doors that it was a sad, sad time. In spite of their sadness, however, former students got together and had a homecoming to celebrate their accomplishments at dear old Douglass. There was a motorcade, followed by a banquet. A former student, Dr. Arthur Shropshire, was the speaker. Mrs. Anna Diggs, the only living student who had graduated in the 1800s was honored. "It was unfortunate that Douglass had to close her doors, not out of desire, but out of design—one the blacks had no say in," Mrs. Jones said.

Mrs. Jones was director of Hannibal's Head Start, and after a retirement that lasted less than a month, she became a sales representative for the *Hannibal Courier Post*, where her presence made a positive difference in terms of coverage of African American contributions and cultural events. She is now working with the foster grandparents program in several northeast Missouri counties, and she continues to be very active in her community. Her daughter Valerie Shaw was the first African American to hold a professional position at a Hannibal bank. Shaw was employed there for ten years before transferring to a Columbia branch, where she has been named vice president and branch manager. Her responsibilities include managing consumer loans, deposit product sales, and teller operations of the bank.

Mrs. Lillian Jones, who graduated from Hannibal's Douglass School, is still interested in education. She now works with the foster grandparents program in northeast Missouri counties. (Courtesy Mrs. Jones)

One of the stories that Mrs. Jones told at a gathering in Hannibal was about how her family came into possession of a famous recipe and developed the business that supported the family for many years.

∾

If you are wondering how my family supported us, they were business people, starting with my grandparents. We lived near the railroad tracks, just below Arch Street, the area they called the bottoms. My dad used to tell us that there was a Mexican who came to the door asking for food from my grandparents. In those days such people were called hobos. It seems as though my grandparents would feed several hobos a day who knocked on the door for a handout.

Well, after the Mexican ate my grandparents' food, having self-respect, he needed to prove he was not a begger. So he offered something in return. And that's how we received the recipe for the McElroy hot tamales. So when my family serves our hot tamales, we're continuing and protecting a family tradition started by our grandparents some one hundred and thirty years ago. They are popular with our family, but we also have regular customers. Some of the customers were children when my parents used to sell the hot tamales out on the street.

I have one customer that mails them to her children in New York. Once a jeweler offered me a diamond ring for the recipe. Now, I love diamonds, but the recipe is a family secret, and we will make sure that it remains a secret passed down from one generation to another. We were always told by our parents, and I guess they were told by their parents, to never give the recipe away, because if we ever needed some extra money, we could always make and sell hot tamales. That is how we raised money for one of my grandsons' tuition. One of the restaurants lets us have a Hot Tamale Day. We raised enough money on one day and one night for that first semester's tuition.

We make hot tamales for special occasions, and I was so happy that my mom wanted to and did help us when she was living. My mom, whom we lovingly called "Muddy," died in 1987 when she was one hundred years, six months, and twenty-four days old. My mother used to cook pigs' ears, hot tamales, chicken, and other goodies, and my brothers would take a stand with a sterno stove, make a shift steam table, and sell those foods on different corners. One brother would be on the west side, while another would be on the south side. Besides doing all this cooking, my mom took in washing and ironing. We would hang the clothes out on the line, and if you hung a sheet by a pillow case, you were in trouble. She wanted all the sheets hung on the line and all the pillow cases together. Everything had to look nice for the people passing by.

I had a great childhood, and I grew up with the knowledge that I had to give back to my community. My favorite project is the Douglass Scholarship fund. We don't just give them away either. We look at grade point averages, community involvement, and character. Not one black student ever received the Louis Armstrong Award, no matter how talented they were. My niece Marla McElroy played for many of the events and for the jazz band, but do you know, she never got that award.

∽

Mrs. Louise Jean Dixon Williams and her late husband, Harold Williams. Mrs. Williams told her granddaughter Angela many stories of her early life and shared memories of her parents and grandparents.
(Courtesy Angela Williams)

Angela Williams is one of the youngest storytellers among us, but she is descended from one of the oldest black families in northeast Missouri, the largest African American family in Hannibal and one of the most enterprising. At age nine she performed with a girls' club I organized in Hannibal, and later she was my apprentice in the master apprenticeship program sponsored by the Missouri Folk Arts Program at the University of Missouri. She has become a popular storyteller at private and public events, recalling stories her grandmother told her as a child and her own experiences.

∼

My grandmother's name is Louise Jean Dixon Williams. She was born at home in Palmyra, Missouri. Dr. O'Neal delivered her, and he also delivered her brothers and sisters. When she was little, she used to play with her homemade toys, bird's nests, and mud. She loved to go fishing with her mother and help with the garden. Her family planted pear trees, cherry trees, apple trees, peach trees, and pear trees. They also raised chickens. She said every Sunday they knew they were going to have chicken. She remembers her mother taking the chicken and spinning it round and round until the head came off. Then she remembers seeing the chicken still running and jumping around without a head until it died.

One of her favorite memories was of climbing a tree and getting an egg from a bird's nest. She would crack the egg and cook it on the sidewalk. She used to go and look for pennies, and when she came across one she would go to the candy store, Bailey's Candy Store. When she came in the man would say, "Oh, here comes my little chocolate drop." She said she loved it and was tickled that he said that to her. But when her parents found out, they didn't like it.

Her school, called Lincoln School, was segregated. There were two floors with three rooms on each floor. One teacher would teach grade levels 1–12. The same teacher taught English, Math, Science, everything. My grandmother had three people in her class. When the bell rang for class to begin, the first thing they did was pray and then recite the pledge of allegiance. At noon they had lunch, and then classes would continue until four o'clock.

When grandmother and her siblings went to school, they rode in a black Ford car driven by their father called "Tin Lizzy." The school was six miles from their house. Their father would drive them toward school for three miles, and then Old Tin Lizzy would break down and they would have to walk the additional three miles. Tin Lizzy did this in the summer and winter. "The car just didn't care," Grandmother said. She said that going to Hannibal back then was pretty special, like going to New York. As a child, she had never heard of Quincy, which seems strange since it is right across the river, but they didn't have transportation.

She said her mom and dad's transportation was the horse and buggy when they were growing up. What she remembers about her parents is that her dad worked from 7 a.m. until 7 p.m., and every Friday he would bring home a sack of candy, which was a big thing. Her mother would make everything from scratch, like bread, ice cream, and cake. She said the thing she remembers about her grandma was that she ironed all the time. She used to take in clothes and iron them for money. She said she doesn't remember her grandpa ever working outside of the home. He would do handy work around the house all day.

When her grandfather came inside from work, he would say, "Ma, I'm hungry."

But her grandmother would say, "There's some bread on the shelf. If you want it, go get it yourself DUN DOO," which means "and that's that!"

Her grandfather would get upset and wait right there until she fixed him something to eat. Then they would laugh about it and enjoy one another's company.

Some of the remedies they had were drinking castor oil once a week and wearing a poultice pouch on their chests to keep from catching colds. They could only take a bath once a week, which was on Saturday. They also changed underclothes once a week. (I bet them underclothes could walk when they took them off.) Not only did they only bathe once a week, but they had to use the same bathwater. Her mother would place the tub next to the hot stove, which was one of those round pot-belly ovens with a pipe that went through the roof. She said she was very careful not to bump her bottom on the stove and burn it. After each person bathed, her mother would pour more hot water in the tub but would never pour out the used water.

There were no indoor toilets, and she said she used to hate going outside, especially in the winter. She said their coats never got cleaned, and they even used them as blankets at night to sleep under. The discipline at home was being put in a dark basement, and she said they didn't get spankings but they got BEATINGS! But she didn't get a lot of those.

Today my grandmother does not have to worry about transportation, sleep with her coat, or any of those things because she is very well-off. She spoils me by giving me the things that I want and I am very happy about that, even though I would love her anyway.

～

Angela also tells about her own childhood, growing up in her family's funeral home in Hannibal.

～

There is a huge, white, foreboding, twelve-room, wood-frame house in Hannibal, Missouri, that has more than thirty windows. There are no curtains or shades on the windows, and the house is deserted. It sits on a hill just above the Hardee's fast food restaurant located at the intersection of Highway 61 and MM. I would guess that the house is now over one hundred years old. It was home for my family and me, and it also served as my father's funeral home.

The house has several levels. We lived on the second floor. At the bottom of the stairs from the second floor down to the first floor there is a hall that leads to a door opening that doesn't have a door. This opening led to what was once the funeral area, where the casket with the body, a space for mourners to view the body, and a place to sit for the funeral service were. During our stay in the house, my father hung two long red drapes that substituted as a door. For all I know, they may still be there. I can tell you with certainty that when we lived there those drapes moved in many different directions—side to side, back and forth, without the help of any strong wind. I imagine that because of the size and age of the house there might have been drafty areas, and that would explain the movement of the drapes. But sometimes the drapes moved when there was no draft.

When we first moved there it was exciting to me because there were so many rooms in the house to investigate, but my excitement was soon replaced by fear, and my wandering days were cut short after I saw my first ghost. It was on a day when I was looking for my parents. I went down the stairs, walked

Angela Williams of Hannibal with her son De Vonte. (Coggswell Collection, courtesy Angela Williams)

down the hall, opened those long red drapes, and stepped into the funeral parlor area. My feet stuck to the floor, my hands gripped one of the drapes, and my eyes almost popped out of my head. I felt freezing cold as a large shadowy figure rose up out of the casket and reached out to grab me. I let out a blood-curdling scream, let go of the drapes, which seemed to make it possible for my feet to move, and ran up the stairs. I jumped in my bed and pulled the covers over my head. By the time someone came to rescue me, I had wet the bed. In fact, I wet the bed every time I was in it, after that day, and it didn't matter if it was day or night. There were other incidents of ghost sightings in that house, even though I was the only one that saw them. My father would say, "Angela, it's the living that you should fear, not the dead. The dead won't hurt you." I was not convinced. I had never been frightened or chased by a living person.

My parents had to admit that no matter how warm the house was, there were times when the temperature would drop

Gladys Coggswell telling stories at Hannibal's Eugene Field Elementary School, 1992. (Coggswell Collection)

to an unexplainable freezing low in one spot or another. After much trauma, drama, screaming, and hiding on my part, my parents finally decided they would either have to move or have me committed. We moved, and I never saw another ghost or wet the bed again.

For a long time after I first began to drive, I would make every effort to avoid driving by that intersection. I would go to any Hardee's but the one located at Highway 63 and MM. I still have vivid memories of musty smells, creaky floors, and shadowy figures darting after me. My parents still own the house, but no one else has ever lived in it since we moved. Do ghosts still live there? I believe they do, and it is probably for that reason that the house remains deserted by those of us who are among the living.

∼

# 3

# Bowling Green

Bowling Green in Pike County is perhaps best known as the home of James Beauchamp Clark, known as "Champ" Clark. His statue welcomes visitors to the town, and information about his career is readily available. Clark moved from Kentucky to Missouri in 1875 and first taught in Louisiana. Although he was a southerner and admitted that he was "a Southern man in feeling and in thought," soon after his arrival in Missouri he watched a trial in Louisiana and wrote in his diary: "learned that there is no justice for the negro in this country."

Clark won a term as congressman from Missouri's Ninth District in 1892, lost the next election in 1894, but won again in 1896, and served until 1920. An eloquent orator, Champ Clark became nationally known as he traveled the country as a Chautauqua speaker. In the presidential election of 1812 he won strong support for the nomination of the Democratic Party for president, but he did not gain the necessary votes, and Woodrow Wilson won the nomination and the presidency. Clark served as Speaker of the House until his death.

Accounts of the settlement of Pike County and other northeast Missouri counties show that African American artisans and free men were there long prior to the Civil War, but not much had been recorded about their achievements, nor of the contributions of the slaves that

Father Augustine Tolton was born in Ralls County, Missouri, in 1854, of slave parents who lived on adjoining farms and who married in St. Peter's Catholic Church in Brush Creek, Missouri. When the Civil War started, his father left to join the Union Army in St. Louis and his mother walked to Hannibal with her three children and crossed the Mississippi River to Quincy, Illinois. Educated in Quincy and Rome, Father Tolton is the first known black Catholic priest in the United States. He died in Chicago in 1897 and was buried in Quincy. (Courtesy Tolton Papers, Bremmer Library, Quincy University Quincy, Illinois)

were brought to the area from Kentucky and other southeastern states. It was in adjoining Ralls County that one of Missouri's most famous African Americans was born. His mother, Martha Jane Chisley, was born in Mead County, Kentucky, in 1833 and at age sixteen came to a farm about nineteen miles southwest of Hannibal with slaveholders Stephen and Susan Elliott. Susan's stepfather had given Martha Jane and four other slaves to his stepdaughter as a wedding present to take to Missouri with her.

According to Margot McMillen in her biography of Martha Jane Chisley included in the book *Called to Courage*, Martha Jane married Peter Paul Tolton, a slave belonging to a neighboring family. Her husband left to join the Union in the confusion of the beginning year of the Civil War, and she left the Elliott farm and walked to Hannibal with her three children. There, with the help of a Union soldier, she obtained a canoe and rowed across the Mississippi River to Quincy, Illinois, escaping, according to family lore, in spite of shots fired at the boat. Martha Jane Tolton's son, Augustine Tolton, was educated in Quincy and Rome and "became the first nationally known African American priest."

Ralls and other counties along the Mississippi River in northeast Missouri drew many slaveholding families from Kentucky and Tennessee in the years before the Civil War. The slaves brought many of their customary practices with them, and one tradition that continues a tradition in many rural and urban communities is the West African practice of deriving medicines from roots, herbs, and other curative plants. In hours, days, weeks, and years of interviewing older African Americans in northeast Missouri, I have heard many accounts of how leaves, roots, and barks were brewed to make tea for medicinal purposes. Nature's products were used to correct indigestion, locked bowels, lumbago, spasms, and the plain old common cold. The remedy I heard about most often was the "asfidity" bag. "Asfidity" is the folk term for asafedita, a resinous material obtained from certain plants of the fennel family, especially *Ferula assafoedita*. It is acrid and bitter. According to William "Jerry" Grimmett, it "downright stinks." He should know. He had to wear an asfidity bag to school to ward off catching a cold. As he put it, "We didn't catch colds. We didn't catch nothing. Those asfidity bags scared off everything but the cold weather."

Mr. Grimmett (most folks call him Jerry) is a homegrown northeast Missourian, born in Bowling Green. In 1946, home from the service, he built the house he now lives in. His sister Frances lives next door in the house that was built by their grandmother. Our interview with Jerry Grimmett took place in the sanctuary of the White Rose Baptist Church in Bowling Green as part of a series of public programs sponsored by the Missouri Folklore Society and the Missouri Arts Council.

During Mr. Grimmett's talk, he passed around two documents relating to his life: his birth certificate, which gives his name as

"Unnamed Grimmett," and his discharge from the Colored CCC, which states that he was "Honorably Discharged . . . by reason of Expiration of Term of Enrollment for the Convenience of the Government," March 25, 1941. The company commander, Carlyle H. Staab, signed his discharge certificate. Mr. Grimmett's story begins with his grandmother, as he told how it was when he was growing up in Pike County.

～

My grandmother was a slave in Cyrene, Missouri. When she got freed she came to Bowling Green. She built her house, and then she met and married Jerry Grimmett, my grandfather. Granddad had been a slave too. They had three sons, Forrest, Frank, and Curtis Grimmett. My grandma always had money. I don't know where she got it, but she always had money. Her son Forrest was a chief cook on the Union Pacific Railroad. He died out there in Omaha, Nebraska. She wanted to bring him home. She took her son Curtis, her oldest son, out there with her. He wasn't married. He didn't have a family. Grandma Betty couldn't read or write, but she paid his way to Omaha, her way to Omaha, to bring her son back to be buried. She brought him back, his wife back, and his daughter back here. She paid all the fares. Like I said, she always had money.

My granddaddy was a caretaker at an apple orchard. He didn't have no education, couldn't read or write, but he could count pretty good. When Grandpa was older, Roosevelt set up the social security system. It was called the old age pension. Grandpa got eleven dollars a month. I'd go to the mailbox and get his check and bring it to him. Every month he'd tell me to open it up, and then he would ask me what it said. Every month I would tell him, "Eleven dollars." That was all he ever got. He'd put his X on the check and tell me to take it up to Randolph's, the neighborhood store, to cash it. I'd bring the money home to him, and he would sit there and count about fifteen or twenty minutes over and over. After he got it all counted he'd say—he'd send me up to Summercamp's Pharmacy, the drug store, for a pint of Dixie Dew. That's whiskey. I was about twelve years old, a little fellow. Summercamp would put it in a sack and give it to me, and I'd bring it back to Grandpa. He'd open it up and give me a little taste of it. Then he would say to me, "Now look, this stuff will make you drunk. This is not good for you. It will make you drunk and a drunk man is no good to you or anybody around you. So you can't fool with it too much."

Grandpa had been a good man and we had a good family. If one didn't have, the other one did. Nobody went wanting and everybody worked hard until they was either too old or dead. Dad worked on the short-line railroad, Hannibal to St. Louis, in the 1920s. That was the name of the railroad at that time. He made about twenty cents an hour. My dad had to work because he always had babies. There was eight of us all together. My grandmother was a midwife most of her life, an old-time midwife. She didn't see fit for young women to have children and be gittin' out of the house in three days, going around, hitting the ground. Walking on the ground was a no no, and all the things that women do today—they didn't do that. She seen fit for them to protect their bodies. They had to wear a belly band around their waists, so that they wouldn't lose their figures. Most of the people in this neighborhood she delivered. She didn't deliver me though.

I don't know why, but she didn't deliver me. Dr. Wilcoxen delivered me, March 10, 1921. They hadn't decided on a name for me the day I was born. Dr. Wilcoxen didn't come back, and nobody could get to town to Dr. Wilcoxen's office to get my name to him. Mom was there with me. Dad was on the railroad, couldn't afford to take a day off, and Gramma was taking care of Mom. We didn't have a car. We didn't have a telephone. At that time we didn't have electric lights. I guess Dr. Wilcoxen decided, "Ah, they ain't got no name for him, he ain't nothin' but a little darky, he ain't go'n' mount to nothin' no how. I'm sendin' this in to Jeff City." So that's what he did.

When I got to working on the Clarence Cannon Dam up here, I decided I needed to get ready to start applying for my social security so I can get it when I retire. I was going through all these procedures. They was telling me you had to have all these baptismal records, old insurance policy, all kind of junk, you know, to get your social security. So that's what I was doing, working through all these channels. Way before that I had always tried Jefferson City for my birth certificate, and every time it come back, it come back "Unnamed Grimmett." So I'm getting mad then, you know, I'm really getting mad because Dr. Wilcoxen just didn't have—I mean I got to tell it like it is, because that's the way white people was back in those days.

Black man didn't really 'mount to nothing—he was just a tool. Couldn't hold decent jobs back in those days 'cause you was a tool for the system. I kinda halfway gave up on it for a long while. Finally, when I did apply for my social security, I didn't need all that junk nohow. They had quit doing that stuff, insurance records and stuff like that. I went up there to Hannibal and filed for it, and I got it. I got part of my birth certificate here now. You all can look at it—it's gittin' in bad shape.

Anyway that's the way it was back in those days. After I got to be a man out of service, I got to working on construction, doing pretty good, making pretty good money, anywhere from sixteen to twenty dollars an hour, why I said a bad word about him [Dr. Wilcoxen]. "You ought to see me now, you old so'n so." That's what I said. But he was dead. I just couldn't—it was just one of those things that was really hard for a man to have to take.

I put my age up to nineteen so I could join [the Colored CCC]. I wasn't by myself. A lot of people was doing it. The United State was in a massive depression at that time. There was very few rich people in the United States. The Vanderbilts—they had money, but most of the people didn't have nothing. Everybody was desperate. We had this opportunity, so I went.

I stayed two years and two months. First place I worked through the CCC was at Washington State Park, fifteen miles outside of DeSoto. We started building a dining lodge that went across a stream. We quarried stones for it. We shaped the stones into building stones by cutting them into chunks with stonecutters, chisels, and sledgehammers. All the work was done by hand. It was hard work, but the work we done still stands. That's a nice building down there. I was down there about two years ago, in 1997, me and my kids and grandkids. First time I'd been back since I left from down there.

Next we went to Mark Twain State Park. There was controversy there. The state of Missouri had purchased about fifteen hundred acres—land from the farmers up there. They had heard about us. Well, a group of white people up there didn't want us up there 'cause we were black. They didn't want us. Another group—they sort of wanted us, so they chartered a bus, came down there to Washington State Park to look at our project. They were really impressed. So they got us.

We had a special dinner on Sundays for the CCC men and the local people. Those people who didn't want us up there didn't want to eat with us. Of course our company commander was a white man. He was a good man. He told them, he said, "Now looka here, I'll feed you, but you got to eat with these people, with my people. I'm not making nobody give up their seats for anybody. That's just the way it is. You wanna eat, Okay. If you don't, there's the road."

So those people started coming, bringing their whole family. They didn't have nothing so they just kept coming back. So he fed them. But he didn't put us behind nobody. He made us all feel good. Made us feel like we was somebody, because most of us had went through this ordeal which degraded you. Everybody liked him.

I broke my arm on the eleventh day of November 1939, went to Jefferson Barracks, and didn't get out 'til April. I guess they just lost me—wasn't nothing the matter with me by then. All I needed was a haircut.

Mr. Jerry Grimmett recalled his years in the "Colored CCC," when he helped construct the sturdy stone buildings in Washington State Park. (A. E. Schroeder photo)

I went in the service in 1943. I got out in 1945. I served my country in World War II. I was awarded two bronze stars for campaigns in Normandy and northern France. I have three overseas bars and one victory bar. I was an expert rifleman and traveled around competing in shooting events. I was good because I could see good—can't see nothing now. Then I came back home, to Bowling Green. I wanted to get some jobs with contractors in Bowling Green, and they would not hire me. I went to school in St. Louis to learn the carpentry trade. Finally Mike Quinn in Laddonia gave me my first chance to use my trade. I helped to build FHA houses, mostly in northeast Missouri.

～

Mr. Grimmett and his late wife, the former Margaret Hendricks, had two daughters. Dawn lives in Bowling Green and works at the

William Grimmett went into the army in 1943 and served until 1945. He was awarded two bronze stars for campaigns in Normandy and northern France, three overseas bars, and a victory bar. He was an expert rifleman and was chosen to compete in marksmanship events.
(Courtesy William J. Grimmett)

men's correctional facility there. Brenda lost her life after a long struggle with lupus. Although he officially retired after working at the Clarence Cannon Dam, Mr. Grimmett still receives calls to consult on carpentry projects. He is actively involved with the National Association of CCC Alumni and with church activities. He shares his stories with students and for special events. He is a proud, independent man, who really doesn't need a birth certificate to know who he is. He knows his name and history.

4

St. Louis

As historians have noted, migration has been one of the defining characteristics of black life in the United States since the beginning of the forced migration of Africans to the New World. When European explorers moved up the Mississippi River in the early 1700s, another forced migration began, with slaves brought up from New Orleans to work in the mines west of the river in present-day Missouri. Slave labor from the South helped build the frontier towns of Ste. Genevieve and St. Louis and, later, the early settlements established along the Missouri River. In the early 1800s, owners of plantations in the southeastern states began to move west to find new land and establish farms in northeastern, central, and western Missouri. They brought thousands of slaves to work on the hemp and tobacco farms that developed from the Mississippi River west to the Kansas border in a migration that lasted until the end of the Civil War. After emancipation, many of these former slaves migrated to the cities, including St. Louis, hoping for better lives for themselves and their families.

In the late 1870s and early 1880s, African Americans who had remained in the South after the Civil War began a migration north to protest the increasing loss of the political rights they had gained for a short time after the war. These emigrants, individuals and families known as "Exodusters," traveled upriver from states along the Mississippi on the way to Kansas, where leaders hoped to establish all-black communities. Often arriving in St. Louis without the means to travel farther, Exodusters found a black community in the city that came together to help them, whether they wanted to continue to Kansas or decided to remain in the city.

Another "Great Migration" of black people from the South started in the 1890s and continued during the first half of the twentieth century. These waves of migrations—from the first slaves brought by the French founders of St. Louis in the late 1700s and their descendants, to later immigrants drawn by opportunities for work—have resulted in large and vibrant communities of African Americans in the city, with, among them, many who not only brought traditional family customs but preserved and treasured these practices for generations.

During the late 1980s I had the opportunity to interview several older St. Louis African Americans through a project called Eldertel. Under the direction of Dr. Marilyn Probe, Eldertel was designed to preserve the cultural heritage of the participants and at the same time boost their levels of literacy and self-esteem. When I was growing up, the older people in our family were highly revered. Respecting one's elders was a way of life, and I was not too surprised when these St. Louis elders turned the tables on us. As so often happens with field research, it was the interviewers who received the educational and cultural boost. It became clear that these proud, dignified elders, most in their seventies and eighties, had no self-esteem issues. They had all been through the school of hard knocks and had graduated with high honors. They had come this far by faith, mother wit, tenacity, and, like their counterparts in northeast Missouri, herbs and home remedies.

Most of their families had migrated from the South, many from Mississippi, and they had arrived in St. Louis "on a wing and a prayer" in the mid-1930s. Along with their stories of their journeys and their former homes they told us of remedies their families had used for childhood and other illnesses.

Mrs. Catherine Clemmons's family had moved to St. Louis from Hayti, Missouri, in the Bootheel. She said that when she was young and had children, she did everything her father taught her because that was what she knew.

∼

I believe that you can get an education, like reading, writing, and math, but in your home you live according to how you was raised. I remember people of all colors came to our house and my daddy would lay his hands on them. Then they would go right back out in the field and work some more.

My father believed in stewing down an onion and honey, right from the bees in the country, and he'd put all that in a pot—castor oil, little bit of sugar (honey more than sugar), and he would add a little whiskey to it. In the winter when it was raining and wet, we could get it every Saturday. We would work real hard on Saturday to get that, because we would get us a white coffee cup of that every Saturday night.

He would mix up a little Black Draught stuff and put that in the tonic. He would stew it on the stove until it would get real syrupy. The honey made it sweet. We would get a buzz, and we would laugh and play a lot. We never was sick—never out of school like other children. My father was a good man, a smart man.

∼

Mrs. Icey Gardner was born in 1909. "I am one of nine children that I know of—six females," she said. "I was born in the field and raised up in Jackson, Tennessee, prior to moving to St. Louis. I was raised on a farm, and I remember picking cotton, wringing chickens' necks, and killing hogs. As a child, I hated to see cotton grow. I knew that was going to mean hard work for me in the fields." Mrs. Gardner remembered how her mother cured flu with corn shuck tea.

∼

In 1920–1921 everybody in Missouri came down with influenza, and they were all dying. Sometimes two or three in a family died from it. All my people got down with that flu—everybody but me and my mom. I guess I was about seven or eight years old. We had to put pallets on the floor. They all came into one room where we could take care of them by one big fireplace. It was wintertime. I had to do all the working so I wanted to get sick, too. Iron teakettles, we had iron teakettles. I put them shucks in them. I'd take the shucks off the corn and twist it around the teakettle, then get that teakettle full of water and hang it on the fireplace. We'd cook some all day—have some hot all day. We wouldn't give anybody any cool water. Every time they wanted water, they had to drink the tea instead. That was the only thing that got them up—corn shuck tea. We'd just take the shuck off the corn, put it in a pot, boil it, and drink the juice. It tasted bitter and nasty, but nobody who drank it died from the flu. We saved them all.

~

Mildred Grice was born on October 4, 1917, in Tulsa, Oklahoma, and came to St. Louis with her family at age seven. "My mother was an Indian from a tribe in Utah," she said, "and she did domestic work. My father was colored. He was a brick carrier or a hod carrier. To tell the truth there wasn't as many sick people as there is today, so there was no reason to have too many cures. Fresh air isn't as good as it used to be. There is a lot of stuff in the air that gets you sick these days." She told us how her mother used potatoes to cure frost bite.

~

Did I ever tell you about frost bite? I think it was Irish potatoes they used. My kids would come in from playing outside for a long time, and their feet and hands would be so cold. My mother would rub their toes and heels with the potato, which was sprinkled with salt. She did this for my oldest son because he got it bad one time. She would just slice the potato real thin and put it on top of the frost bite. My mother believed in the power of the potato. Whenever any of us had an ailment, she would rub a potato over our head. After

Carole Shelton was born in St. Louis and remembers both her grandfather and her father as wonderful storytellers. An educator and professional storyteller, Carole began her career as a seasonal park ranger at the Arch, the Jefferson National Expansion Memorial, incorporating folktales, legends, and myths into her historical presentations. Her storytelling later expanded into historical portrayals and personal, inspirational, and original stories. She shared a story about "Brer Rabbit" and one of his tricks.

that she would bury the potato and wait for us to get well. We got well, but I don't know if it was from the potato.

Any way I never tried that one, but I guess I would if I got really bad off sick. We never went to the doctor, though. All my friends who went to the doctor are dead now. Isn't that something?

∽

We agreed that was really something, and I discovered that the St. Louis eldertellers themselves were really something.

Carole Shelton was born in St. Louis and grew up in a family of storytellers. She encourages others to "explore, share, and experience the power of storytelling," and she shares a favorite family story, "Brer Rabbit and Little Roy Green," and with it the joy of visiting her grandfather and hearing his stories.

∽

The minute our mother told my brother and me that we were going to spend the night with our grandfather we would begin chanting, "Roy Green from New Orleans don't eat nothing but turnip greens," and this would continue until he arrived in his car, which he called Betsy.

We called our grandfather by his first name to the dismay of every adult who heard us say, "Roy." My grandfather was Roy Green from Texarkana, Texas, and was born about 1894. He was short in stature, barely five feet tall, but he could tell some stories. Roy was on his way to Chicago in 1921, having left Texarkana hurriedly as there was considerable racial tension and several lynchings had occurred there. He stopped in St. Louis to visit his sister and decided to stay. Several months later he sent for his family, his wife, Hattie Howard of Hope, Arkansas, and his daughter, Bernice Lillian. My grandmother died shortly after I was born.

My brother and I were the apples of our grandfather's eyes. Roy took us for rides in his car, taught us to fish, and how to roll cigarettes. He had a very special flavored coffee he brewed himself. Roy told us the reason we couldn't taste his special coffee was it would make us black inside. I don't drink coffee to this day. Roy was always telling us stories to entertain us when we stayed with him. Some mornings we would have fried salt pork, pancakes, and Brer Rabbit maple syrup. That maple syrup bottle with the pictures of Brer Rabbit on it would always remind Roy of the times he tangled with that rabbit. Sometimes Roy would get the best of Brer Rabbit, and sometimes Brer Rabbit would get the best of him. Well, this is the story of "Brer Rabbit and Little Roy Green" as my grandfather told it.

It was one of those right fine summer mornings in Cooter Hollow, Tennessee. Folks were up and about the business of the day. Now down the road came Brer Rabbit, stepping mighty high, just a-whistling and a-chewing on a long piece of grass. Folks were mighty surprised to see him out and about so early in the morning. You see, Sis Green had threatened to brain him within an inch of his life with her cast-iron skillet if she ever caught sight of him. Folks were talking about Sis Green carrying around her cast-iron skillet day after day, everywhere she went, just hoping to catch sight of that rabbit!

OLE RABBIT AND HIS WIFE.

"Brer Rabbit" had many names. In St. Joseph, Missouri, he was known as Rabbit or Ole Rabbit, and he was never up to any good.

This is an image of Ole Rabbit and his wife from Mary Alicia Owen's *Voodoo Tales*. (Drawing by Juliette Owen; State Historical Society of Missouri, Columbia)

Now, folks nodded politely at Brer Rabbit, and he nodded back, but they kept a watchful eye on him. You see, just like the sun rises in the east and sets in the west, that rabbit was always up to some mischief. On down the road stepped Brer Rabbit until he came to the fork in the road. He stood there a minute, studying like, chuckled, and then turned towards the fishing hole. Brer Rabbit made his way down the narrow path leading to the lake. He took a seat under a large shady tree and leaned back to relax. Then Brer Rabbit laughed out loud to himself about the last time he was there. You see about a month ago he had come across Little Roy Green at that very spot. Little Roy, as folks called him, had invited Brer Rabbit to sit a spell, because he wasn't having much luck fishing. He had promised his momma, Sis Green, they would have fish for dinner. Little Roy was feeling mighty low because he hadn't caught not one fish.

Brer Rabbit sat a spell just watching and chewing on a piece of grass. Little Roy still wasn't getting any bites. Finally, Brer Rabbit suggested they move to a different spot and see what happened. Well, they moved and nothing happened.

Then Brer Rabbit leaned forward and said, as his nose twitched, "The best thing to catch fish with is tufts of hair."

"What's that?" asked Little Roy. Brer Rabbit reached out and patted Little Roy on the head.

"Oh, we can get some hair from the barbershop," said Little Roy.

Brer Rabbit said, "Ain't got time for that, you got lots of hair."

"My momma will skin me alive if I let you cut my hair."

"She won't even notice after you show her all those fish."

Little Roy thought a moment and said, "Okay."

Brer Rabbit took out a pair of scissors and cut a plug of hair out of Little Roy's head. "See, that's not a lot. Now mix it with a little of that dough you got there and put it on your hook."

Little Roy put the hair and dough mixture on his hook and threw his line into the water. By some miracle of miracles, a fish jumped on his hook. Little Roy took to whooping and hollering and jumping up and down. He was overjoyed with catching that fish while Brer Rabbit was dumbfounded, speechless, and surprised. Little Roy carried on like it was the biggest fish ever caught! Brer Rabbit just rolled his big eyes back in his head and gathered his senses.

Now Brer Rabbit decided this was a perfect opportunity to have some real fun. Little Roy was so anxious to catch more fish, he threw out his line again, but this time nothing happened. He waited and waited. Finally, Brer Rabbit suggested he needed a new tuft of hair and dough.

Well, Little Roy thought about it for a moment. Maybe he

was right. So he let Brer Rabbit cut another plug of hair out of his head. He put that new mixture on his hook and threw his line into the water, and sure enough, by some miracle of miracles, a fish jumped on his hook. Little Roy carried on like he was a fishing fool, but when he put the same mixture back in the water—no fish.

Now Little Roy studied on the matter. He was in the second grade and second graders know everything. Old hair mixture—no fish, new hair mixture—fish. It seemed pretty clear to Little Roy what he needed to do.

Brer Rabbit said, "Little Roy you are a right smart feller, yes indeed, and quick-witted too."

Little Roy was delighted with his newfound smartness. He let Brer Rabbit cut and cut plug after plug out of his head to catch fish. Now the sun was high and it was very hot, and Little Roy's head was getting awfully warm. He started to sweat and felt right faint. Little Roy sat a spell but that didn't help. He thought he ought to go home so he packed up his fishing pole and all his fish. He offered Brer Rabbit some fish and thanked him for his help. Brer Rabbit declined the fish politely.

Brer Rabbit and Little Roy walked to the main road and said their goodbyes. Brer Rabbit went one way. Little Roy went the other. As Little Roy walked away, Brer Rabbit turned to watch him and was overcome with laughter. He was laughing so hard his face started to hurt and he dropped to his knees. It was the funniest thing he had seen in a long time! Little Roy, stepping down the road with his chest stuck out carrying all those fish, and his head looked like a plucked chicken, bald spots here and there all over his head.

Down the road through Cooter Hollow walked Little Roy with all his fish. He was right pleased with himself and took to strutting. The town folks spied his plucked head as he walked by and took up cheering and whooping. Little Roy thought they were cheering and whooping about all the fish he had caught, so he just smiled and waved as he strutted with pride down the road! By the time he arrived home, half the town was following behind him, carrying on loudly.

Sis Green and her lady friends came out into the yard, and Little Roy raised the fish to show her. A broad grin came over her face as she looked at her son with all those fish. But the crowd was pointing and whooping at him. When Sis Green put on her spectacles, she screamed and fainted dead away. The town folks got seriously quiet and began to quickly move away from Sis Green's house. Her lady friends helped her to her feet and back into the house.

Poor Little Roy was so embarrassed about his head that he stayed in the house for almost two weeks. His momma shaved his head, but some spots didn't grow back. Sis Green had always been a good church-going lady with no violent tendencies, but she let it be known, in no uncertain terms, that she meant to do great bodily harm to that rabbit if she came across him.

The day had been big fun, and the folks in Cooter Hollow had a good laugh at Little Roy's head. And as for Sis Green she would forgive Brer Rabbit sooner or later, probably much later, or maybe not at all.

Back up to the main road stepped Brer Rabbit, just a smiling to himself about that day. He looked both ways down the road, trying to decide which way to go. Just then, in the distance, he spied Brer Possum coming down the road. He looked like he was dancing!

"Well, I think I'll go this way and see my old friend Brer Possum," said Brer Rabbit to himself.

On down the road stepped Brer Rabbit just a-whistling with mischief on his mind. As for Little Roy Green he would get even with that rabbit and you could count on that.

∾

Although African Americans migrating north as slaves or free people brought their folk traditions and hard-won skills for surviving to Missouri, they had long realized that education—being able to read and write—was the key that would allow their children to have better lives than theirs. Northern missionaries who came to St. Louis to teach after the Civil War wrote of the eagerness with which former slaves welcomed opportunities for schooling for their children and the hardships they were willing to endure to pay for it. Even before the war, missionaries, some Catholic orders, and others had managed to provide some education for blacks, both children and adults.

A well-known black minister who had managed to establish a school for black children in St. Louis was called John Berry Meachum. Born into slavery in Virginia, Meachum had become a skilled carpenter and had earned enough money to buy his freedom and that of his father. Migrating to Kentucky, he married a slave and followed her to St. Louis when her owner moved west. In St. Louis he established a barrel-making business and bought his wife's freedom. A deeply religious man, he founded the first African Baptist church in St. Louis and soon began to offer classes in the basement of the church to teach reading and writing.

In 1847 the Missouri legislature passed a law against educating black children, whether slave or free, and Meachum created a floating school on a steamboat he owned anchored in the middle of the Mississippi River, where federal law prevailed over state law. He ferried the children to the boat on a skiff, and according to Gary Kremer one of his students was a young boy who would go on to become famous himself. James Milton Turner, born in St. Louis County in 1839, attended the famous Meachum "floating school" and later went to Oberlin College. After the Civil War, Turner traveled throughout Missouri for the Freedman's Bureau to visit the schools established for African American children and found most poorly equipped and the teachers lacking in adequate skills themselves. Turner later taught in the first schools for black children in Kansas City and in Boonville.

Few black teachers were available for a number of years after the war, and some parents kept their children home out of fear they would face discrimination from white teachers, but in 1875 the St. Louis school board established a black high school with a normal department to train black teachers. Selwyn Troen reports that in the 1877–1878 school year, when black teachers were first hired, school enrollment

This bust, commemorating James Milton Turner's contributions to education, is in the Morgan Street Park in Boonville. When Missouri passed a law in 1847 making it illegal to teach black children, educator, minister, and businessman John Berry Meachum created a floating school on a steamboat in the middle of the Mississippi River so that he could continue to teach children to read and write. James Milton Turner, who reportedly attended Meachum's floating school, studied at Oberlin College and, after the Civil War, traveled throughout Missouri as the secretary of the Missouri Civil Rights League reporting on conditions in schools for black children. He taught in both Kansas City and Boonville schools before his appointment by President Ulysses S. Grant as minister to Liberia. (Photo by Richard Schroeder)

increased by 35 percent. In St. Louis, as elsewhere in Missouri, black teachers created a "second home" for children, a place where they could learn "reading, writing, and arithmetic," even though their books were secondhand and pencils, paper, and other supplies had to be shared.

Storyteller Mettazee "Mett" Morris, a graduate of Mississippi College, has homes in St. Louis and Quincy, Illinois. My grandmother used to tell me, "A heap sees, but a few knows." Mettazee both sees and knows.

Mettazee Morris, an internationally known storyteller, recalls her own educational experiences in a newly integrated school in Mississippi. She shares a moving account of her Uncle Johnny's life as a teacher in St. Louis along with one of his favorite stories. (Courtesy Mettazee Morris)

She has a large repertoire that includes family stories, and one of the stories she tells is about her uncle Johnny Vincent Gray, who taught in St. Louis's public schools for twenty-eight years. Mettazee's account of her Uncle Johnny's life and the lives of others in her family provides a rare view of the African American experience before and during integration. At the same time it celebrates the achievement of a man who became an inspiration to his family and many others at a time in American history when such quiet leaders made tremendous contributions to the survival of their families and communities.

～

My Uncle Johnny was an athlete. He played college football at Jackson State University in Mississippi. After college, he was drafted into the National Football League to play for the Dallas Cowboys. At the end of training camp, he injured his knee and was cut from the squad, but we were all still excited and very proud that he had even been drafted. We celebrated his honor and shared in the joy of the brief privilege and experience he had earned.

As was typical of my uncle, he shared the signing bonus dollars with everyone. He shared with my grandmother, his brothers and sisters, and of course with me. In 1969, with hopes of a football career behind him, Uncle Johnny headed to St. Louis to begin his teaching career. I was not surprised. He loved children and was always very caring. Even though he wasn't much older than I was, he seemed much older and very wise.

Uncle Johnny was the next to youngest of thirteen children. I called Uncle Johnny's mother, who was my grandmother, "Dear Dear." Her name was Thomizene Gray. Jeff Gray Sr. was my grandfather's name, and I called him "Grandpa." Besides raising their thirteen children, they raised me, too. Actually it was Dear Dear who raised us, because Grandpa had lost his eyesight shortly after their last child was born. My grandmother would get up at daybreak in the mornings and cook breakfast for all of us. She would then walk ten to fifteen miles a day to go to work and come home again. Uncle Johnny was a big help, but our getting an education was more important to my grandmother than any help we had to offer.

I remember the first year of being integrated into the school in Clinton, Mississippi, where I grew up. It was Uncle Johnny who helped prepare me for the experience. The night before, he came home from college to give me moral support and offer his words of wisdom. I remember he said to me what I had often heard my grandmother say to my uncles and aunts, including Uncle Johnny. "Just be yourself and you won't have to see the colors of the rainbow through nobody else's eyes."

So that is what I did. Still, I was unprepared for the shock of being given a typewriter with blank keys on the keyboard. All of the white kids had keyboards with letters, numbers, and symbols. I was mad as a hatter. I didn't know what I expected my grandmother to do when I told her about the keyboard, but she didn't make a big deal out of it.

She asked me if they gave me a book with a picture of a keyboard that had everything on it, and when I said they had, she said, "Well, then, that's all you need. You're smart enough to study that book, learn where everything is, and practice, practice, practice. Just make believe you've got the same kind of typewriter the other kids have."

I did what she said, and Uncle Johnny would come home from college on weekends and help me memorize the lineup of the letters, numbers, and symbols that were on the keys in the picture in my book. Even then, he was a great and patient teacher.

When it came time to take the speed test, I was the fastest typist in my class. I was the only one who could type seventy-four words a minute. Uncle Johnny tossed heaps of praise my way, and I felt mighty good. "That's my Mett Tett," Uncle Johnny would say, and that was good enough for me.

That is the worst memory I have of white school. Any other trouble I encountered was of my own doing. We were taught by Dear Dear to love everybody, and I did, even when I decided I had to deck them. I wasn't afraid of anything or anybody, and I didn't look for trouble, but I never liked to see anyone mistreated. One of the black girls in our class had asthma, and one of the white boys, a high school football star, picked on her. I believed it was my business to straighten this situation out. One day when he was teasing her, I grabbed his jacket, ripped his letter off, and decked him. I warned him that he better not bother her again.

We both had to go to the principal's office. The principal sent the boy home. He said he knew that I didn't start the problem, and that he wasn't going to have anyone picking on anyone in his school. He sent me back to my class. After that, we didn't have any trouble, and I didn't have to protect anybody. I could concentrate on my schoolwork more, and I was a good student. When I think back about those days, I realize how amazing and bold Mr. Ray, our principal, was when it came to trying to do the right thing. I believe it was his attitude and behavior that influenced the teachers to eventually—sooner or later—at least act like they wanted to teach us. I wonder what he would have done if he had known that I was given a typewriter with a blank keyboard. I overcame that, and I was popular with the other students. I knew I could sing better than anyone in the whole school, and they knew it too.

I sang with the school choir, and every time we performed, our principal insisted that we sing the gospel song "Ain't Got Time to Die." To the credit of our principal, if the school that was inviting our choir to perform did not want black students included, then our choir didn't sing there. To the credit of the white students, most of them didn't want to go and sing without us. We had a great sounding choir—too bad some people missed hearing us because of racism. It was their loss. Uncle Johnny often came to hear us. He would be in the audience—just beaming. That made me work harder at singing my heart out. I wanted my family to be proud of me, and they were, and they made a point of letting me know they were.

Uncle Johnny worked hard too, and we were always really proud of him. During his career in St. Louis, he worked at Beaumont High School, Sumner High School, and Mark Twain School as a coach and physical education teacher. He believed in the power of education, was devoted to his students, and made a difference in their lives. At that time there were not many opportunities for black students to get a higher education after high school. Uncle Johnny would load up his car and drive students across the States, literally depositing them in black colleges. He helped them get the limited scholarships that were available to blacks and mentored them through college graduation and job placement. He did this almost every year for twenty-five years, and he said that not one of his students ever let him down. He had a 100 percent success rate, maybe because he really believed in his students. He cared and he showed it.

My uncle sent money home to my grandmother from every paycheck he ever received. He really loved his family, and he loved St. Louis. He always wanted family to visit him so he could show us the highlights of the city. He was a member of Central Baptist Church and served on the usher board. He was proud of his usher ensemble, complete with white gloves. It gave him great pleasure to take visiting family members or friends to his closet and show them his white uniform. In July of 1992 he hosted our family reunion in St. Louis. Family came in from Detroit, Nebraska, California, Mississippi, Oregon, Tennessee, Chicago, and Georgia. For us, he was definitely the "host with the most."

Uncle Johnny cultivated his own "family" in St. Louis. It seemed as if he knew everyone and everyone always seemed happy to see him. Wherever we went, even to the grocery store, people knew who he was. It is no wonder that everybody loved him. He was kind to everyone. One of my uncle's best friends was Mr. Lawrence Walls. Mr. Walls said of him, "Johnny was a real special person. He would do anything for anyone and never expected anything in return." My uncle never had any biological children, but he was father to lots of children, young and old. When his girlfriend died of cancer, he was like a father to her children. When one of his best friends was very sick and snowed in, the friend's wife was frantic with worry that she would not be able to get her husband to the hospital. She called my uncle for help but couldn't reach him. She decided to go outside and try to get her car out herself. When she opened the door, she was surprised to see that Uncle Johnny had shoveled the driveway and the walk. He took his friend, whom they did not expect to live, to the hospital.

Ironically, the following year, on October 13, 1997, Uncle Johnny's friend was still alive, but my wonderful, precious uncle died of kidney failure at DePaul Hospital. While on this earth, Uncle Johnny obeyed the Master's will. He committed his life to his calling, nurturing his family and everyone who shared his space with genuine love, acceptance, and patience.

He talked the talk and walked the walk with dignity, sincerity, and compassion. Every day I try to live up to his standards.

One of the ways I try to do this is by telling stories that will positively impact the lives of others. I first heard this story from Uncle Johnny when I was younger. I thought he had made it up himself, but later I learned the story was based on one of Aesop's fables. I just know my uncle told this story about "The Black Crow" to some of his students, especially the ones he escorted to black colleges. I don't quite tell it the way he did, but I tell it my way.

There is a saying, "Wise as an old crow," and the reason for this saying is a known fact that crows are the most intelligent birds. Flo, being true to the crow's reputation, was a master problem solver. Other birds came to her with their problems and always left with a solution. One summer there was a drought. There wasn't a drop of water anywhere and no sign of rain.

Half dead from thirst, Flo went looking for some water. Not too far behind her was a group of moocher birds. They figured that Flo was so wise, she would find water and they could mooch some of it. When they saw Flo swoop down, they swooped down too. There, right in front of their eyes was a pitcher that had some water in it. With what little energy the thirsty birds had, they knocked the crow out of the way and got closer to the pitcher first.

Each bird put its beak into the mouth of the pitcher. That's when they realized there was a big problem. Only a little water was in the pitcher and not one of them had a beak long enough to reach far enough to get a drink. After a few tries, they gave up and started grumbling. They even got to calling Flo names—called her a stupid ol' has-been. They took their little selfish thirsty selves and flew off in a huff—left poor Flo there to dry up and die.

But like I said, crows are intelligent birds and Flo was no exception. She looked at that pitcher and looked at the ground—looked at the pitcher again, picked up a pebble and dropped it in the pitcher. Mustering up as much strength as a weak and thirsty bird possibly could, Flo kept picking up pebbles and throwing them in the pitcher. When it seemed like she was about to pass out, she forced herself to pick up another pebble. She dropped it into the pitcher. That did it. The pebbles took up so much space that the water had no choice but to rise up to the mouth of the pitcher, right where Flo could easily take a drink of water. Ooh, Ooh, Ooh! That water was soooo good.

Once her thirst was quenched and her life was out of danger, she thought for a quarter of a minute about the birds that had called her a stupid ol' has-been. She gave a hearty crow chuckle, stretched her wings, and flew to the nearest tree, where she took a well-deserved nap.

At the end of the story Uncle Johnny always said, "The wind blows, the road bends, and this is where my story ends."

⁓

Mett Morris's account of her experiences growing up and her Uncle Johnny's life as a teacher and role model for many St. Louis children has life lessons for those who listen to the stories of the elders. One story I heard as a child, I heard later on in Frankford from Mrs. Camie, and then I also heard the same story from a janitor in St. Louis. I often conclude my own storytelling programs to children with it.

⁓

This story is about two little boys and an old man. The old man used to sit on his porch all the time, rocking, and patting his foot, and smoking his pipe, as sometimes old men will do. And these two little boys used to like to go and tease this old man. And they'd get so mad because he knew everything. There was nothing they could ask him, nothing they could talk about, that he didn't already know about.

Now these two little boys did not have an ounce of respect

in their souls. So they were determined they were gonna make this old man wrong. They got together one day and one of them said to the other, "You know I am sick and tired of that old man. I am sick and tired of him always thinking he knows everything."

And the other one said, "Well, I know what we could do."

And the first one said, "What?"

That other one said, "Go get us a bird. We gonna put it in our hands. And we'll go up to that old man and say, 'Say old man, you see this bird we got in our hands?' Ummm, ummm. And we're gonna ask him whether it's dead or alive. If he say it's alive, we'll crush it and kill it! If he say it's dead, we're gonna open our hands and let it go!"

Well the other little boy, he goes, "Ah, ha, ha, ha, ha, ha! That sounds good to me. Good, good, good, good!"

So they got a bird. Went up to the old man, just laughing, oh, they could hardly contain their laughter. They just knew he was gonna be wrong, and they couldn't wait to see his face when he was wrong.

"Old man! You see this bird here we got in our hands? Is it dead or is it alive?"

And the old man took his pipe out of his mouth, rocked a little, patted his foot a little, and smiled. He said, "Chillen, it's in yo' hands."

∾

# 5

# In the Bootheel

A good part of the African American migration north to Missouri in the early twentieth century resulted from the invasion of a small bug into the cotton fields of the South. As early as the first decade of the century, folksong collector John Lomax had heard what he called the "Ballad of the Boll Weevil," sung by black tenant farmers and farmhands working in the fields.

> First time I saw de Boll Weevil
> He was settin' on the squah
> Next time I saw dat Weevil
> He was settin' everywhah
> Jes' a-looking foh a home, looking foh a home.

It was not long after the appearance of the boll weevil that many black families in the cotton states were also "looking for a home." John Handcox, the "Sharecropper Troubadour" and organizer for the Southern Tenant Farmers Union, sang of their plight:

> Homeless, homeless are we
> Just as homeless, as homeless can be

Missouri's "Bootheel" counties in southeast Missouri developed a plantation culture as the boll weevil invaded the South and sharecroppers moved north to find work in the cotton fields west of the Mississippi River. (Gerald Massie photo; courtesy Missouri State Archives)

We don't get nothin' for our labor
So homeless, homeless are we.

As displaced tenant farmers from the South moved to Missouri, the Bootheel region, thought to be above the "Boll Weevil Line," gradually developed a plantation culture not unlike that in the South, according to Thad Snow, who had moved from Indiana to Missouri in 1910 and bought a thousand acres in Mississippi County. In his autobiography, *From Missouri*, Snow wrote of the changes that occurred in what he called "Swampeast Missouri" after the introduction of cotton farming in the early 1920s. After black workers had come into the area, farmers of southeast Missouri became "rarin' back planters." Snow had observed earlier that it "is necessary to know how rich we are in order to understand why we have so many more poor people than other farming areas in the Midwest." He eventually had twenty-three sharecroppers

John Handcox, labor organizer and "troubadour" for the integrated Southern Tenant Farmers Union in Memphis, came to the "Swampeast" Missouri farm belonging to Thad Snow of Mississippi County when his life was threatened in Arkansas. He stayed for several months. (Mr. Handcox was in Columbia during the commemoration of the fiftieth anniversary of the Roadside Strike; courtesy Western Historical Manuscript Collection in Columbia and St. Louis and Claudia Powell)

and tenant farmers on his own farm and more on another farm he had bought, but according to John Handcox and officials from the Southern Tenant Farmers Union in Memphis, he was sympathetic to the union. Handcox, who stayed for several months on the Snow farm in 1936 after his life was threatened and he had to leave Arkansas, wrote a song to him:

> He says to me, something for labor ought to be done
> And you are perfectly welcome to go on my farm . . . .
> Then he asked me what else he could do
> To help put our labor movement through.

After a trip to the Southwest and Mexico, Snow wrote, "I had satisfied myself that the landowners of the Delta had merely followed a pattern of behavior in respect to their tenants and croppers that had become widespread and accepted practice in every commercial farming area I knew. In my view it amounted to a national scandal."

The Missouri Sharecroppers Roadside Protest in 1939, organized by the Reverend Owen Whitfield of Mississippi County, brought national and international attention to the plight of sharecroppers in the Missouri Bootheel. It was commemorated in an award-winning film, "Oh Freedom After While," produced by Lynn Rubright with the support of the Missouri Humanities Council. (Western Historical Manuscript Collection at the University of Missouri–St. Louis)

The tenant farmers of the Bootheel, led by the Reverend Owen Whitfield, organized a Sharecroppers Roadside Strike near Sikeston in January 1939, and the night before the strike, those planning to participate in the event that was to bring unwelcome national attention to conditions in the Missouri Bootheel sang verses from a Handcox song at meeting in Reverend Whitfield's church: "Raggedy, raggedy are we. . . . Hungry, hungry are we. . . . Homeless, homeless are we." Handcox had left Missouri by the time of the strike, but he recorded his songs for the Library of Congress, which has preserved them.

My own first glimpse of a cotton field came during 1994–1995 when I was assisting in a research project in southeast Missouri sponsored by the National Endowment for the Arts. Long before setting foot on Missouri soil, however, I had heard about cotton picking in Missouri from Uncle Pete, who claimed to have Missouri roots. Uncle Pete told me that when he was "down in Missouri" he was very poor. He tried to make money by picking cotton. "But I got cheated every time. Couldn't make a dime. I don't ever want to see no more cotton unless I am wearing it," he would say. Uncle Pete had conveyed his memories of Missouri sharecropping through his stories, one an old folktale with many variations that is still told at African American family reunions and storytelling sessions. When I tell it, I just let my Uncle Pete take over.

～

John sharecropped for Old Boss, but whenever he sold his cotton, it seemed like he come out on the short end, always owed Old Boss, never come out ahead, couldn't even break even. If John made seventy-five dollars on his cotton, Old Boss would get to figuring and say, "John, 'cordin' to my records, look like to me you owe me 'bout one hundred and fifty-two dollars and eighteen cents."

John would protest and say, "Why that's more'n I get for the cotton myself."

Old Boss would pat John on the back and say, "Now don't you go worrying about it. Just gimme what you got, John, the seventy-five dollars, and we'll let the rest go on the book. Then we can settle up next year."

Every year John owed Old Boss more, and as time went on, settling up was nowhere in sight. John got tired of this debt cycle and decided to turn the tables on Old Boss. While coming back from town one day, he met Old Boss on the road. Old Boss asked him how much he made on his cotton sale. John looked right mournful, lowered his head, and told Old Boss that he hadn't done too well. He explained that there was a duck epidemic in town and he had come down on the drop side of the deal.

He reported, "I sold the cotton all right. I had the money in my hand, but here come all the ducks and got it all. They

Evelyn Pulliam. (Courtesy Evelyn Pulliam)

deducks for putting my wagon in the wrong place, they deducks for the rotten bolls, they deducks for taxes an' one thing an' another. Yep, deducks got it all, so I reckon we gon' have to settle this thing up next year." John giddyupped and left Old Boss standing on the side of the road in the dust scratching his head. When he got home, he took his cotton money out of his pocket and put it in his stash. "Okay, Ol' Boss," John said. "Now we's almost settled up."

⌣

During my visits to southeast Missouri, I was fortunate to have several interviews with Evelyn Pulliam of Kennett, who told me of growing up in the Bootheel as the plantation culture there was changing.

⌣

I grew up in North Lilbourn, a little village of about seventy-five African American families, where practically everybody was equal. We were all poor. Nobody realized we were poor as children. We just thought it was—we were normal, like everybody else. In this village where we lived there were people who worked as sharecroppers, people who worked on the farm, a few people who cleaned houses and did other little chores, but there wasn't a lot of labor and not a lot of money flowing around.

Few people had cars, and everybody had to walk. That was the common understanding. If you wanted to go to town or if you needed to get somewhere, you started off walking and hitchhiked. That's what I remember about my town, about the other people and the families around. There was this situation that we, the families, knew what everybody had because there was carpooling, they call it carpooling now—going to the grocery store. Nobody went to the grocery store by himself if he had a car. There were always five or six other people in the car. I can remember my mom and several other ladies going to do the grocery shopping and they would leave, you know, they didn't take children with them because there was no room to take us if parents had to go. And then they would come back with the groceries for the week, or the next two weeks, all packed in the trunk and it was exciting to see the vegetables and the fruit.

The families, they all—I don't remember anybody not helping someone when we were there. Everybody pitched in and helped. I can remember my mom and other ladies in the community, when an older person was sick and couldn't take care of the home the way she should or fix food the way she should, they would get together on Saturday morning and clean the house. We had one lady, we called her Mother Edmunds because she had been there for a long time. Her husband had died. And she was very, very old—she walked on a stick and couldn't get around, but Mother had a house and she was still independent. Things that she couldn't do for herself she would put off. And the ladies didn't want to see Mother live in filth or be worried about getting work done. So there were about six or seven, and we would all go with them because we would have to do something, carry mops, pick up paper, or whatever. Do something—work in the yard, burn the trash. They kept us busy, and they would clean her house. She would cry, and they would clean, but she would be thankful. They would wash her clothes, they would fix up food so that she wouldn't have to cook for a few days. And this they did on a regular basis for her because she wasn't able to do it for herself. And soon—I remember when she became unable to live by herself, one of the others, it was just a couple, took her in, and she stayed with them until she passed. So there was a lot of caring and sharing, and as children we didn't have time to worry about what the other one had because it was all just about the same.

I was talking to my mom and another lady about when they used to comb my hair. We used to go to school and we'd wonder how big a hurry our moms would be in because every morning we'd get our hair combed. Some would have three, some would have four braids. It's according to how much time you had, but you had to have your hair combed every morning before you went to school. So we would count and say, well she had more time, she put four plaits on my head this morning. If she didn't have enough time, she put two or three. Unless your mother braided your hair when we were young that meant she was lazy and she didn't want to comb your hair every day. Very seldom was it any fancy hairdo, except on Sunday, we would get our fancy hairdo.

I went to school at first in a one, well, it wasn't a one-room school, it was like a house. It was a big white house with at least three rooms. I think it held first, second, and third grade. And I remember those teachers over there. I remember how they used to—we used to do fun things, you know, we didn't have to worry about this integration problem back then. We never even thought about it. Because our teachers were black, all the students we went to school with were black, just like we were, and we hadn't begun to realize what was on the other side of the world.

At least we didn't in North Lilbourn because the only white people who came to visit us in the village was the doctor and the insurance man. The insurance man would walk from house to house collecting ten and fifteen cents on policies. And we would see that after he made the rounds in North Lilbourn, he would head toward Catron, which was like five or six miles down the road. This man would walk all the way there, in the country, and collect insurance. He didn't have a car. He walked. Now that was one white person we saw on a regular basis. And then the doctor, Dr. Chestine, he was the doctor that used to come and visit us in the projects. He made his rounds. Every so often he would come by and he'd visit all the kids. He'd visit us and make sure we were all in health and check us out. And I think he charged—Daddy said sometimes he charged a quarter. He said, "We paid what we could and that's what he took." He said that was the only doctor that would come out and visit us at the time.

I can remember my sister having diphtheria and Dr. Chestine told us we were quarantined. And my dad—in fact there were several houses under quarantine at the time. And these dads had to go to work, and my dad was wanting to get out of the house because he was not a person who could sit in the house all the time. So he sat there when Dr. Chestine told him, "Okay, you gotta stay in, you can't be out visiting, you can't be out playing, you need to stay in the house to keep these germs quarantined." Well, my dad looked around, and he looked at us, and he took it [the little white rag to show the house was under quarantine] off the house and went to work. Well Dr. Chestine, he came back, he put it back on. And my uncle was a schoolteacher, he'd take it off because he couldn't afford to miss school, he said. And he would go in his room when he came home (we were not allowed in there after that) and shut the door, and he kept it shut—like he was going to keep all the germs out of his room because he shut off one door. We were not allowed to go in or near it. And that's how we survived. I don't know if anybody ever stopped doing what they were doing when they found out about the quarantine. I know they didn't at the Thomas household. Everybody went to work. We were the only ones grounded. I had to stay out of school and seems like I was out quite a while. I missed two sessions—one because of being ill on my own and one because of the diphtheria.

So I barely was in school the first two or three years. But then things began to change. During the time I was growing up, there was a time when people went on the harvest. When they stopped sharecropping and couldn't chop cotton or pick cotton to make money, people started going on the harvest to make money. So, you know, we had to split sessions. So they continued to split sessions because some people would take their families with them. So we had some families to go and some families to stay. Now, on the harvest, they would pick potatoes, green beans, tomatoes—all kind of vegetables and everything, but these different families worked in different areas and what they would do to save their money was whoever worked in the potato field brought in potatoes enough for everybody up there. Whoever worked tomatoes brought in enough tomatoes, who had cucumbers brought in cucumbers. Or whatever vegetable they had. They shared it all.

Sharecropping was on its way out, and those big ol' things called cotton pickers came, and that's how the cotton was picked. There was a cotton field right behind North Lilbourn Village. One day, one of these cotton-picking machines started on the far side of that field and worked its way over close to where we lived. When we left that morning for school it was on the far side, but when we got back from school that evening it was close to the house, and we were all fascinated with watching it.

Well, the closer we got, we saw something as we were turning the corner—hundreds of rats. All those rats were leaving the field. Their home had been in the field but now they were cleaning up the field. The rats had to go. They were frantic and so were we. The big machines run them out of

When mechanical cotton pickers became available, the resulting loss of jobs and increasing poverty led to a crisis for which there seemed no solution. (Gerald Massie photo; courtesy Missouri State Archives)

their homes. They had to find themselves another home. We children ran to our homes, and the rats ran right into our homes too. Our little village looked like the Pied Piper of Hamlin had been there. The rats were running all over and invading the place. They were so big—they were huge to us. They had lived in the fields and had plenty to live on out there before the cotton pickers came. Now they had made up their minds to move to our North Lilbourn projects. Everybody was trying to figure out what to do about this situation. We could tell when poison was being put out because there was a stench that nobody could get rid of. The smell of dead rats was thick in the air. And let me tell you, they were in every house. Nobody could talk about anybody else. I swore, however, that we had the most rats. Because of where our house was located, the first house near the field, it was the one they would get to first.

After that families started moving up north, because the children were getting bigger, and some of the dads wanted to make a better life, and they could get jobs in factories. So one of our neighbors down the street moved, took his family and moved up north. And they rented their house to a family we had never seen before or heard of. We don't know where they came from, but I remember this little boy. He was a bully. And his name was Boots Strickland. Boots wore army boots, and he wore a white shirt and jeans all the time. His mom put him in white shirt and jeans. And he would get out in the dirt and he'd roll around in that shirt. We called him Boots because he loved them big ol' clompy boots. I don't even know if them boots ever fitted his feet or not. But Boots was our bully, and he bullied every child out there in North Lilbourn. Oh, we was scared of Boots. Because we didn't know where they came from. We said they came from waaay out in the country somewhere because they hadn't been around other people and didn't know how to act. They were not nice. They were always—why, they would just pitch stuff right out the back door. Would just burn my mom up. Burn her up. She'd say, "Look you could take it to the trash can." But they wouldn't do it. They'd just pitch it right out the back door.

And then Mom would holler at them. Ooh and they would fight, and if we would look at them they would want to fight us. That was our first experience of really being around a bully, and you know, to get to the bus we had to pass by their house. And we were always scared to go past Boots and them's house, because it was so many people. So much going on. And we were told when we were little, "Now you're not to go over there anymore because we don't really know them." Because we knew the other family that had moved out. But this family was different.

Now, down from Boots Strickland's house was Ms. Mary's house. And Ms. Mary was a foster parent. And she would take in foster children. Why, we never knew who was going to catch the bus from Ms. Mary's house from one time to another. And you know what? They always seemed to bring these children at night. We never saw them bring them in the daytime.

They would bring them at night. The bus driver would stop in the morning, and we'd see who would come out of Ms. Mary's house. Ms. Mary had one of those houses with lots of room. Ms. Mary was a widow woman. Ms. Mary made her living taking care of foster kids. Ms. Mary was a nice lady, she made them behave, and she always welcomed us when we come down to visit her. And we went to her house. When we went in Ms. Mary's house, it was different from our house because it was so big. Well, for a table—we had never seen a table as long as the one Ms. Mary had. What she had done, because, you know, we had to make do and find what we could, she had taken two picnic tables and pushed them together and covered them with sheets and made a tablecloth. That's just how many little children she had. At that time, I don't know if there was a limit because I do believe at one time she had over twelve children living with her in foster care. And that was very strange because we didn't understand about foster care and why these parents were losing their children. That was one of the first beginnings of the system that we knew. We knew that sometimes parents would die and leave their children, but we couldn't understand why the system was taking children from them. We didn't understand about that. In our school, you know, we always expected to see someone from Ms. Mary's house. And we did until she moved to St. Louis. And that was a great loss because that was a wonderful house—wonderful. We always knew someone new was gonna come out of that house. It was very exciting.

I went to an all-black school 'til I was in the eleventh grade. And my experience with the all-black school was quite different from what it was with integration. We had plays, we had contests, we had to get up and do recitations, and we had to perform. Our teachers cared about our learning. We had everything in that environment that a child needed to feel good about himself or herself. So we integrated in 1969–1970, and all that stopped. It was a terrible time. It was a quiet time. It was the students and teachers in the white school that affected my heart and mind. We didn't have anything to do at the new white school in Lilbourn.

On the first day, the students were crying and clinging to each other, consoling each other as if they were at a funeral. It was the first time in my life that I felt rejected. I didn't feel inferior though, because I thought something was wrong with them for acting that way toward us. We didn't know how to treat them. The teachers ignored us for the most part. They had the black kids sit on one side of the room and the white kids on the other. The white teachers never even looked at us. They turned their backs to us so that they wouldn't have to see us when we raised our hand. Eventually, we got the picture and didn't even bother to raise our hand. It was a terrible time, and our parents didn't make it any easier. Our parents' main concern was that we act right. They assumed that because the school was white, it was right, and that we would be treated fairly. They assumed that if anything went wrong it would be reflected on them. As a result, we didn't even tell them what we were going through.

I was discussing it with Mom. She said, "You know, we never really thought about . . . we were concerned about you all and we wanted you to act right because we didn't want nothing to fall back on us. . . . We should have been more concerned about how they acted." And she said we made a lot of mistakes during that time because we thought that since we were one of the last ones to integrate they would be more accepting. WRONG! I saw classmates that were average students because their parents were not—you couldn't say they were just illiterate, but they didn't have school training—but they were determined that their children were gonna be—go to school—I saw them leave school during my junior and senior year and not graduate because of minor, little, minor things that should not have even counted.

And I saw the young men in my classroom tested in their manhood against the teachers. They were always acting like the boys were usurping their authority. Teachers especially singled out the black boys in the classes, and when they couldn't take it any more, they dropped out. I saw them leave. I saw them not graduate. I saw young ladies get confused, not sure of themselves. Trying, some of them, trying to reach out, but they were reaching out in the wrong way to the wrong people and they got hurt. I saw a gradual decline in the number of my classmates, the ones I had grown up with. I saw withdrawal. We withdrew into ourselves. We were the only class that I knew that had two presidents, two secretaries, a black one and a white one, because we could not come to an agreement.

Most of my senior year is a big painful blur. What should have been the happiest days of my life were the most miserable, and today I still don't feel as if I was a part of a senior class or a graduation, even though I did somehow manage to stick it out and graduate. It has taken a long time to work through this. But I was determined not to make the same mistake with my children that black parents (including my own) had made with us. I taught my kids about racism and about what to expect. I taught them not to be afraid to stand up and speak up for themselves when they know they are right. I never let them believe that our skin color is the problem. I let them know that racism is an ignorance problem that some white folks have. I let them know that their job was to get an education—something no racist could ever take away once you have it. I told them my version of an old folks' story that I'm gonna tell you. You probably already know this story, the story "Why Dogs Chase Cats."

∾

Once upon a time cats were bigger than dogs, so they captured dogs and forced them to do hard work. They worked the dogs so hard their muscles developed and they began to outgrow cats. So one night the cats called a cat committee meeting to decide how to keep the dogs from getting out of hand. Many made suggestions, but the one that stuck was the one made by Granddaddy Cat, who had hated dogs from the git-go, even when they were small and loyal.

Granddaddy Cat said, "Let's tell them dogs how stupid and lazy they are. Let's tell 'em we'll help 'em get better lives if they try to help themselves, and the only way they can help themselves is to learn to be like us. First thing we got to do is give 'em a test—the meow test.

"We'll tell them that their smartness is measured on how they master the meowing test. We'll make them believe it's our meowing that makes us better than them."

All the other cats—except one, who warned the cats that this plan was wrong and could backfire—agreed to the plan. The cat that disagreed was branded a "dog lover" and hung on a limb by the tail.

When the dogs heard about the meow test, they went to classes taught by the cats in the hope of making higher scores on the test. They went to be tutored by cats. They practiced every day. But no matter how hard they tried, they scored poorly on the meow test. They started doubting themselves and getting mad. They began to fight among themselves but still tried their darndest to be like the meowing cats. One day a fox wandered into the cat village—scared the cats so bad they ran up into the trees as fast as they could go. The dogs were not afraid and held their ground. They found their real voices and began to bark. When their chorus of barking filled the air, the fox made a hasty getaway. It just hurried and skedaddled. It was then that the dogs realized that their bark was valuable. It made them mad at the cats they had once been loyal to and even trusted.

Dogs must have passed this story on for generations because, ever since then, it has become a cultural tradition among dogs to bare their teeth and bark at cats. They chase them up trees and will not tolerate a sound that even resembles a meow. They have no respect for cats. Dogs would not be chasing cats today if cats had not tried to trick them and make them think they were inferior. Maybe dogs aren't so easily tricked today because they know this story. It lets them know they don't have to meow to get respect.

∼

Evelyn reports that she is "grateful that many racial barriers have been lifted." She believes things are changing for the better.

∼

All three of my children, Kenya, Robert Jr., and Andrew have graduated from high school, and they didn't have as many problems as we did. They were very involved in anything they wanted to participate in and not just on the sidelines. Most of their teachers were fair.

They have been leaders and have felt connected to their school and community. Their interests range from conservation to sports and music. They feel good about themselves and are very confident. Their friends are black and white, and my boys are both excelling in college. I am very proud of my children. It has taken a long time for me to work through the hardships and heartache that came with integration. We were brought up to be forgiving, and I continue to strive toward that.

I don't hate anyone for what happened, and I teach my kids not to hate. I know I am doing better because a couple of years ago I received an invitation from some of the white students to attend a high school reunion. I refused to even consider going. Lately I have at least been considering the possibility of going to the next one. Maybe they want to apologize. Maybe they are having a hard time sleeping. I have often wondered how much other blacks, others across the country, suffered during the transition from their familiar schools to a strange and hostile school. I wonder if they too felt like nobody cared. I pray for them. I pray for my former classmates who never graduated. I pray for me. I pray for all of us.

∿

Evelyn has been a resident of Kennett, where her husband was born, for more than twenty-five years. She is a leader in her church, community, and in the surrounding area and has received local and state awards for efforts to eradicate racism.

Loretta Washington, storyteller, speaker for the Missouri Humanities Council, and writer, is now a resident of St. Louis, but many of her stories tell of her early years in the little town of Wardell in southeast Missouri, and of her great-grandmother who told her stories. After a long career in bookkeeping and accounting, Loretta Washington, the mother of two and now a grandmother and great-grandmother, "stepped out there on faith," as she says, to share her stories of her early experiences in the Bootheel. At the time they shared their stories with me, Evelyn Pulliam and Loretta Washington did not know one another, but like Evelyn's family, Loretta's had migrated from Mississippi to the Bootheel in search of a better life. Her parents migrated farther up the Mississippi River to St. Louis, but she spent her early years in Wardell, and she speaks movingly of Ellen, her great-grandmother, who told her stories.

∿

When you look at a map, you see that the state of Missouri is shaped like a boot. The small town of Wardell can be found in the boot heel of Missouri, in Pemiscot County. I spent part of my childhood, or my formative years as they are called, in this small country town with my great-grandmother and my grandmother. During that time those two women showed me unconditional love, laying the strongest foundation that anyone could lay for a child. To this day I often reflect back on my days with them.

My great-grandmother Ellen—or "Mama," which is what everyone called her—was born a slave on a plantation in Tennessee on March 2, 1860. After the end of slavery, my family moved from Tennessee to Mississippi. Back then, girls got married at an early age, and Mama was not an exception to this rule. In Mississippi Mama met my great-grandfather Cornelius Walker. About one year later, on January 24, 1878, Mama and my great-grandfather were married. On January 3, 1900, their twelfth child, my grandmother, was born. My great-grandfather passed away soon after my grandmother's birth, and Mama became the head of our family.

My family, like most African American families in the early 1900s, were sharecroppers, and like most, they did not make any money at it. The bosses often cheated the sharecroppers out of their meager earnings. So in the early 1930s, after many years of sharecropping and getting deeper and deeper in debt, my family and another family slipped out of Mississippi late one night. Both families came to Missouri looking for a better life for their children. They worked first in a little town called Swift, which no longer exists. Some years later my family moved to the nearby little town of Wardell.

In 1949 my parents separated and later divorced. My brother and I were sent to live in Wardell with Mama and my grandmother. At that time they lived just outside of town in an old wooden house near a gravel road. At the tender age of four, I had no idea that the time I spent in this small country town would leave such a lasting impression on me. From the time I was five years old, I can remember Mama telling me stories. But my first memories of my great-grandmother were of her old beat-up snuff box that never wore out and her snuff brush. Mama's snuff brushes always came from a small branch of an old weeping willow tree that was in our back yard. I remember this so well because, sometimes before Mama would start a story, she would call me to her and say, "Baby, I think this old snuff brush is worn out. Would you go get me a branch off that old weeping willow tree in the back?" I would run down the steps of the wood porch and run around to the back of the house to the old tree. Then I would stand there looking up anxiously for a few seconds, trying to find just the right size branch. When I thought I had spotted the perfect branch, I would jump up, pull it down, and break off a piece of it. I would run back to Mama and say, "Is this all right, Mama? Is this all right?"

Now, when I think back, I don't care what size the branch was, Mama would always say, "That's just fine, baby, just fine."

Mama would sit down in her rocking chair, cut off a three- or four-inch piece and peel off the green bark. She would start chewing one end of it until it was as fine as the bristles of a toothbrush. Then Mama would go into her apron pocket for her old snuff box to get a dip. She always packed the snuff right in her lower lip. Once this was done she would take her snuff brush and roll it around in the snuff box and place it in the corner of her mouth. Then she would start the story. While this ritual was taking place, I always sat quietly beside her on my little wooden stool. I watched and waited patiently. The wait was always worth it.

At age six I started attending Hodges Grade School, and the stories seemed to get better that year. I can remember getting off the old beat-up yellow school bus and running down the gravel road. The first thing I would do is look to see if Mama was sitting on the front porch waiting for me. And if she was waiting, did she have that look on her face that told me I was going to hear a story that day? Now the school year in the South was different from the school year up north. In Wardell and throughout the South the schools always closed during cotton-chopping and cotton-picking time. Everybody of working age worked in the fields. During that time I had Mama to myself a lot. Mama was too old to work in the fields and I was too young, so we spent a lot of time together and she told me stories.

I will never forget the summer of my seventh birthday. That summer the stories were the best ever. I could have sat on my little wooden stool and listened to Mama tell stories all day long. There was an art to the way she explained the simplest little thing. She would draw you right into the story and you felt like you were a part of it. One of the stories that I especially liked that summer was the one about how my grandmother got her name. My grandmother's full name was May Tankie Belle Walker. Can you imagine having a name like that attached to you for life? The story itself is not funny, but whenever Mama would call my grandmother by all three names, now that was funny. Mama would say, "May Tankie Belle, come here child." Oh, my grandmother would get so mad she would tighten every muscle in her body. She would make this ugly face, like she had been sucking on a lemon, and say, "Yes'em, Mama." My brother and I would look at Mama, then look at my grandmother, and start laughing. We would laugh long and hard, but somehow, even as children, we knew that deep inside she really hated that name.

Well, this is how she got the name. Mama wanted to name my grandmother Tankie, but the wife of the man they were sharecropping from wanted to name her May Belle. So Mama decided to give her child all three names to please the boss's wife and to keep the peace. According to Mama, in 1900, thirty-five years after the end of slavery, the word "freedom" still didn't mean much. So that's how my grandmother became May Tankie Belle Walker. But when my grandmother became an adult and had more freedom, she dropped the May and she dropped the Belle and became Tankie Walker. This pleased Mama and made her very happy, but every now and then, with that little smile on her face, Mama would call to my grandmother, "May Tankie Belle, come here, child." And every time my grandmother would tighten up her muscles and frown like she had just sucked on a lemon.

The storytelling went on for most of the summer of my seventh birthday. Then one day near the end of summer, after Mama and I had been sitting on the front porch for most of the afternoon, she didn't tell me a story. We just sat there watching people, wagons, and old Model-T cars pass by. If someone passed by that Mama knew, they would stop, and as they say, "pass a few words," and then go on their way. But if someone passed by that Mama didn't know, they would just nod at each other. Nodding was a way of saying hello but never passing a word, and the person never stopped walking.

Well, this kind loving woman that I had grown to love so much was about to say something that I would not fully understand until later. Mama looked down at me that day and said, "Baby, I won't be here with you come next summer." At that time I didn't think of Mama as being old or imagine that she would die. I thought that she would always be there. Mama would live forever. Being only seven years old, I didn't understand what she meant. So I looked up at her and said, "Mama, what do you mean?" Mama just smiled at me and started rocking slowly and singing her favorite song.

> When you hear of my home going, don't worry 'bout me.
> When you hear of my home going, don't worry 'bout me.
> When you hear of my home going, don't worry 'bout me. Oh, no.
> 'Cause I'm just another soldier and I'm on my way home.
> Oh, I'm just another soldier, hum hum hum hum hum
> huummmm.

Then, with a little smile on her face, Mama softly said, "Yes, Lord, on my way home."

Well, of course, that afternoon I didn't hear a story. I just sat there, quietly listening to Mama hum and watching her rock as she chewed on her snuff brush. Several days passed with Mama acting like this. Then one morning she woke up and was her old self again. The stories started again, and they were as good as ever. The storytelling continued until the weather started to turn cool. Mama had just finished telling me a story one afternoon near the end of September when all of a sudden she stood up, walked to the edge of the porch, and looked across the old gravel road into the open field. She took in a deep breath of the crisp fall country air. She smiled and looked down at me and said, "Baby, I think it's time for us to go in for the winter. Take your stool now and come on." I picked up my little wooden stool, and she called for my brother, Junior, who was playing in the front yard, to come get her rocking chair and we went inside.

For weeks after that Mama was kind of quiet. She would get up every morning and sit in her rocking chair and rock and hum that song all day. Sometimes I would get my wooden stool and sit beside her. I hoped she would tell me a story, but she never did. Soon after that, Mama started to stay in bed a lot. Then we started to have lots of company coming by to see her. At first it was exciting having company, because they always brought their kids with them, and we played while they visited with Mama. But then the company started to take up too much of my great-grandmother's time, and I didn't like that. When they left, Mama didn't feel like talking to me or telling me stories. When Mama did talk to me, I could barely hear her or understand what she was trying to say. Mama was starting to get so weak she couldn't give me the hugs that I loved so much. Except for her stories, I think I missed her hugs the most.

Soon Mama started to stay in the bed all the time. Every morning I would get up and go to her bedroom door and stand and look in at her. Some days Mama would look at me and smile and wave her hand. On other days she didn't know I was standing there. I knew that something was wrong, but nobody talked about it or explained to me what was happening. I felt so alone. Mama had been my best friend. My grandmother would stop and hug me sometimes as she went in and out of Mama's room. She would tell me that everything was going to be all right, but I knew that it wasn't.

Then late one night shortly after Christmas, I was awakened by a noise in the house. My grandmother had sent for the doctor. Mama had gotten worse. After the doctor finished examining Mama, he stood near the front door talking to my grandmother. My grandmother started to cry, and so did I.

I turned and walked away and went and stood by Mama's door. I had done this many times before, but this time was different. The room was dimly lit because the oil lamps had been turned down. The curtains were pulled tight. Mama's old mirror on the wall had been covered with a black cloth. Silence gathered in the room. Everybody just sat there very quietly.

In the South then, this is what people did when someone was dying. I remembered I had seen something like this before when a friend of my grandmother's had died. Back then, when someone was dying, family and friends would gather. I had been to wakes and funerals, and now this sad thing was about to happen to my family and me. I didn't want to admit it to myself, but I knew about death. Now, for the first time since Mama had gotten sick, I knew that she was dying.

Family members and friends were standing and sitting all around Mama's old iron bed. My grandmother walked past me as I stood in the doorway, and she went and stood near the head of Mama's bed. She stood there holding Mama's hand, stroking it gently, as the tears rolled down her face. From the doorway, I could see Mama, lying in bed, and see her lips moving slowly. My grandmother dropped Mama's hand, turned, and ran from the room saying, "She's singing that home-going song." I turned and watched my grandmother run out the front door. I looked back at Mama again and then ran to my bedroom crying. I cried myself to sleep that night.

When I woke up the next morning, I got up and went to Mama's door to stand as usual, but her bed was empty. Mama was gone. She had passed away that morning around five-thirty. The date was January 14, 1953. As I stood there looking at her empty bed, tears swelled up in my eyes, but I held them back and turned and slowly walked away. I went to my room and sat down and cried for a long time that day. The next few days were not easy for my family and me. Everyone missed Mama, but at that time I thought I missed her the most. We had lost Mama. What were we going to do? Who would take her place? Mama was gone. What was I going to do? I had lost my best friend.

Well, as time passed I accepted the fact that she was gone. I also realized that nobody could take her place. We all have our own time here and our own gifts to give in this world. Mama had her time, and she left her gifts here for us to use freely. I believe that the gift my great-grandmother left me was the gift of storytelling, yes, the gift of storytelling. I miss Mama a lot and I love her as much today as I did that last summer we spent together.

In the spring of 2000, I visited Wardell with two of my cousins. Much had changed; the population then was only 325 people. Half of the town was torn down and most of what was left standing was boarded up. The old cotton gin is all rusted, and machines now pick the cotton that people used to pick. And I heard that they grow rice there now.

I went down the old gravel road that we lived near when Mama died. It hasn't changed very much. As for the old wooden house, at the place where it stood there is no sign that it ever existed, except for the two old trees that sat beside it. But I still felt the need to pull the car over to the side of the road and get out. I stood in the middle of the old gravel road just looking down it and smiling. As I stood there, some of my most precious memories came back to me. I could see the little old wooden house so clearly in my mind. I could see myself as a little girl running down the gravel road after getting off the old yellow school bus. I could see myself looking to see if Mama was sitting on the front porch in her rocking chair. And if she was sitting there, did she have that look that told me she was going to tell me a story today? I could see myself running up the steps of the wooden porch, smiling at Mama, see myself sitting beside her on my little wooden stool. And I could see myself looking up at her, listening to all of her wonderful stories. Most of them were true I believe, yes, I believe they were true.

When you hear of my home going, don't worry 'bout me.

❧

# 6

# Country Schools, City Schools

In recalling their life stories, most African Americans touch on their school days, of learning reading, 'riting, and 'rithmetic in the "old days." Many remember their school experiences fondly, in spite of the problems they faced. At my request Loretta Washington recalled her school days in her country school in the Bootheel and, later, the city schools she attended in St. Louis after she rejoined her mother there.

~

School days in the 1950s and 1960s were different from those of today. I can remember when I first started attending Hodges Elementary School in Wardell. Through the years I've had dreams about that little country school. But in my dreams the school is always much bigger than it really is. In my dreams, it is a big building that takes up a square block, and to walk into the building I always have to go up several concrete steps and open a big double door. Once I'm inside, however, the building is always the same, a small five-room country school.

In my dreams the front yard and the playground area is one big parking lot and all around the building is pavement. I dream there are even painted lines on the pavement for cars

Loretta Washington recalls her childhood and school days in Wardell in Pemiscot County, and attending high school in St. Louis. (Courtesy Loretta Washington)

to park between. In reality that five-room school had a small gravel playground area in front, with a swing. As for the yard back of the building, it was covered with weeds and grass and had no area for us to play.

In the 1950s it was common in African American schools in the rural south for grades to share classroom space. Most of the schools had combined grades because the buildings were usually very small. Most were in poor condition. We were fortunate at Hodges School because we had a small brick building. In 2003, when I last visited Wardell, the school building was still standing. When I first started attending Hodges Elementary School in the early 1950s, we didn't have preschool as we do today. All we had was called "premble," which was our version of kindergarten. In premble we were not taught nearly as much as today's preschoolers and kindergartners learn. At Hodges, premble and first grade shared the same classroom, and in premble we learned to draw and color pictures with crayolas. I can remember we had only a few pieces of crayolas for the whole class. And, yes, I said crayolas; that is what we called them. I didn't hear the word "crayons" until I returned to St. Louis. Back then paper was not as plentiful as it is today, and we never threw a sheet of paper away. It was always reused. First it was used for printing on and then we used it for coloring and cutting out dolls and other objects. After that we still didn't throw it away. We would recycle it for the last time by using it to start fires in the stoves and heaters.

When I went to the first grade side of the room we learned how to say and print our ABCs and how to count and write our numbers up to one hundred. We drew and colored even more pictures than we had in premble. We did not learn reading in the first grade, but the few books that we had were read to us and we could look at the pictures. Two I remember were *Dick and Jane* and *Little Black Sambo*.

In second grade I went to another room, and we started to learn the three "Rs," or the three "R-rus" as we pronounced it back then. When I say we started to learn them, I mean just that. Everything was kept very simple for us. We didn't have a chance to learn or be exposed to the things that the majority of today's second graders encounter. I heard about the three Rs, or the three "R-rus," at an early age, and I knew that they meant reading, 'riting, and 'rithmetic. The adults would always tell the children, "You need to go to school and learn your three 'R-rus.'" My brother and I had returned to St. Louis to live before I realized 'riting and 'rithmetic were not words but stood for "writing" and "arithmetic."

Reading, the first of the three "R-rus," was my first big challenge. In second grade as we started to learn some basic reading skills, we read our first book, *Dick and Jane*. This book told the story of a little white girl and a little white boy who had a wonderful life. Each day was filled with playing and having fun. The book began with "See Dick, see Jane. Look at Dick run. Look at Jane run. Look at Dick play. Look at Jane play." It went on and on with Dick and Jane having all kinds of fun. As a child I always liked the book about Dick and Jane best because they had everything a child could want. To me, Jane had a perfect life. She lived in a nice neighborhood with lots of other big houses in it. Her own home was a nice big house with grass all around it. Everyone in the neighborhood was always dressed up, and they always looked like they were having fun. Every time I read that book I wanted to be Jane. I wanted all the things she had. I felt that if I lived in her neighborhood, I could do all the exciting things that she and her brother, Dick, did every day.

Later that year we started reading our second book. This book had more words to learn. It was *Little Black Sambo*. This was the first book that I owned. Little Black Sambo's life was very different from Dick and Jane's. The book showed him as a little boy with a charcoal black face and body. He had thick bright red lips that always drew attention to his face and facial expressions. Most of the time his face had a comical smile on it. Little Black Sambo's eyes and nose were nothing but white circles in his black face, and he had a bone in his hair. At that time I thought the bone was cute and funny.

The story of Little Black Sambo took place in the African jungle. Unlike Dick and Jane, Little Black Sambo could talk to tigers. An uncontrollable anger arose among the tigers that caused them to destroy themselves. They grabbed each other's tails and refused to let go. They ran around a tree so fast that they melted into butter. The book ended with Little Black Sambo and his family having tiger butter for dinner. I can remember asking my grandmother if we could have tiger butter for our bread.

As children we were taught that Little Black Sambo was a funny story, so we laughed at him. I have often thought that this book represented my first real memory of how I believed African Americans were supposed to be, look, and act. As a young adult, I used to get angry when I thought about Little Black Sambo. In my thirties I let go of that anger; but when I let the anger go, I became a little sad when I realized that as children of the mid-1900s we were taught so little about what life could be for us. I wanted to see and to read the book again and went to the library to see if I could find a copy. I found two versions of the story of "Little Black Sambo." In each version the authors did a more thoughtful retelling of the story. I could feel the compassion that each put into his rendition of the book. I realized that I had grown, I had matured, and I could finally let go of this book.

A few days later, thinking about my years at Hodges School, I found myself thinking again of the teachers we had back then. Our teachers weren't trying to teach us that African Americans lived like Little Black Sambo. They simply used the resources they had available to them at that time. This book was one of those resources. It was a reading tool of that time and nothing else. Little Black Sambo did not exemplify the lives of African Americans. Now I can accept this book for what it was, one of the few reading tools that our teachers had access to at that time. They used what they had to teach us something very valuable. They taught us how to read.

'Riting was the second of the three "R-rus." 'Riting at this stage consisted primarily of learning very simple spelling words and then printing them. They were usually two- or three-letter words, such as "cat," "dog," "boy," "is," "at," and so on.

'Rithmetic, the third of our three "R-rus" at Hodges School consisted of simple addition problems. As examples of 'rithmetic we learned $1 + 1 = 2, 2 + 2 = 4, 3 + 3 = 6$. We were not taught too much more than that. In the second grade we never added numbers that totaled more than 99, and it was okay for us to use our fingers when we were learning how to count. We did this because we didn't always have paper and pencils to use.

In the third grade we started to learn more, but we also had to share all of our books. There were never enough books so that each of us could have his or her own. We continued the three "R-rus," and we started to do additions that totaled over 100. Later that year, we started to add sets of triple numbers. We never got to four numbers, but we learned simple subtractions.

In the fourth grade I went to another room, and we started writing simple words using capital letters. My reading was coming along all right, or so I thought. I could read some books by myself in fourth grade. We continued to do addition and subtraction, and we started to do very simple multiplication. At the end of the fourth grade, I moved over to the fifth grade side of the room. I was finally in fifth grade with the big kids and thought I was doing well in my studies. We continued to learn more about the three "R-rus," still calling them the three "R-rus." My reading and 'riting skills were improving. My 'rithmetic was okay. We started to do more multiplication, but I can't remember doing any division. I spent half of the year in fifth grade at Hodges, and then my brother and I returned to St. Louis to live.

We returned in late 1955 and started school in January 1956. Little did I know of the hurdles that were waiting for me in the St. Louis public school I entered. My biggest hurdle would involve my math skills. In fourth and fifth grade at Hodges, I had never heard of fractions or percentages. Another major hurdle for me was language. I had never heard of breaking down a sentence. I didn't know what a compound sentence was. I knew a little bit about nouns and pronouns, but I didn't know about proper nouns, verbs, adverbs, adjectives, and so on. All these terms were completely foreign to me. To make matters worse, in St. Louis they had an unusual high/low grade system, and my brother and I didn't have any idea what it meant.

The St. Louis school year was divided into two parts. The first half of the school year was called "low," and the second half was called "high." Since my brother and I started in the second half of the year, both of us were put into "high" in our respective grades. I started school in five high and was

scheduled to complete fifth grade by the end of that school year in June 1956. Coming from a small country school, we found our achievement levels were low, very low compared to those of the kids in the city schools. I spent a lot of time in "five high" wishing I was back in Wardell, attending Hodges Elementary School, longing for the safety of the small country school.

Now when I think about the years I spent at Hodges, I realize that we were good students, but the quality of the education we received was not good. This was not because of poor teachers. The low standard of education came from the quality of the educational system in place in the rural south in the 1940s, 1950s, and beyond. Students, teachers, schools, and learning tools were low on the list of priorities for African Americans at that time. We had eight grades in our small school and had multiple grades in each room. Though we got along with each other, and our teachers always seemed to manage somehow, they didn't have much to work with most of the time. At times the teacher would teach both grades the same lesson. At other times our grade would work on an assignment while the teacher worked with the other grade. She would then work with us again while the other group worked on their assignment. This was a typical day for a teacher in a rural south classroom.

Early in my first year in the St. Louis schools, my teacher could see that I was having problems. My brother was also having difficulty. The teachers told our parents about our problems, but I believe a lot of our teachers knew about the poor quality of education in the rural schools. Some had attended rural school themselves, and they knew how little the teachers in the schools had to work with. When school ended in the summer of 1956, I was kept in five high. My math and reading skills were so far below the average level that my teacher was afraid to pass me, fearing that I would not be able to keep up with sixth grade work. My brother was struggling, but he managed to keep up and went on to the next grade. It was hard, but he made it, and we were all happy for him.

When school started in the fall of 1956, my brother was on track in what was called the "low" level in his grade, but I started the fall in five high again, instead of six low. I graduated from grade school in January 1960 because of the low/high system and started high school in January in what was known then as "nine low." We moved in January, so I attended another school. Even though no one at my new school knew about it, I was still hurt and embarrassed about failing five high. During my first year at my new high school, I found out that I could make up the half year that I had lost back in the fifth grade, and I decided not to let that obstacle from the fifth grade haunt me any longer. For several years I took extra classes during study hall, and went to summer school, and graduated from high school in three and a half years, at the same time as my former fifth grade classmates. I knew that my 1956 classmates were not aware of this small milestone in my life, but it was a great personal accomplishment for me, one that I will never forget.

The low and high grade system ended in the 1960s. Now I appreciate the system, for if it had not been in effect in 1956, I would have had to spend another year in the fifth grade. No child wants to repeat a grade in school, and I definitely didn't, not even half a year, but I later realized that repeating the fifth grade was the best thing for me at that time in my life. I had many hurdles to get over besides the problems I had in school. My brother and I had left St. Louis when I was four years old. We returned when I was ten. I had been away from my mother for six years that are crucial in a child's life. My brother and I saw our mother maybe once a year when she could afford to come to Wardell for a visit. We got letters from her often, but I really did not know her when we returned to St. Louis. She had remarried and we also had a new stepfather to get to know.

I had no memory of actually leaving St. Louis, but I had flashes of the apartment we had lived in before I left. Now I was back in this big city that I had left six years earlier. I had grown to know and love Wardell, which was about the size of four city blocks. Uprooted from a small country school beside a gravel road, I was now in a huge three-story school building that was bigger than any building in Wardell and surrounded by busy paved streets. I felt lost and afraid in the big city and the big school. I didn't have any friends, so I spent recess alone most of the time. I was put in a classroom that only had one grade. The students in the city school were more advanced in their studies. I didn't talk the same way, and the city kids often laughed at the way I spoke. They laughed at me when I couldn't answer a question or when it took me a long time to do simple fractions on the blackboard. I was behind at school, I had to try to get to know my mother again, and I had to get to know my new stepfather. During that first year I had a great deal of adjusting to do, but eventually I started to feel more at ease. I made a few new friends in and out of school, and I got to know my mother again.

I eventually began to realize that St. Louis had its advantages. We lived in a part of the city with a confectionary on the corner. The little store was filled with candy, ice cream, potato chips, sodas, and anything else a ten-year-old could imagine. In Wardell we went to town maybe once a week on Saturday, and the grocery store in town didn't have many of the treats that this small confectionary had. I began to enjoy life in the city, but I found I had some catching up to do.

I was in high school before I realized that I had not lost all my southern accent. During my tenth grade year, I raised my hand in American history class to answer a question, and I used one word in my answer incorrectly. The correct answer to the question had the word "people" in it. The teacher embarrassed me by making me repeat my answer over and over. I kept saying "peoples," and the whole class was laughing at me by the time I realized what I was saying wrong. That was the day I really started to watch my language, and as the saying goes I turned that lemon into lemonade.

I did not know at that time that I would some day become a storyteller and a writer. I had no idea I would be traveling down such an exciting road on my journey in life. For many years I had painful memories of that day in school, but I remember how the experience motivated me to start watching my speaking skills. At the time I didn't know it, but a seed had been planted within me. And guess what? Many, many years later that seed began to grow. It has grown and I have matured into a person who always tries to be positive about life, even the lemons along the way. I always had something to say, and in the summer of 1995 the storyteller in me started to blossom. In the spring of 2000 the writer in me started to grow. And as they say . . . the rest is history.

∼

Marlene Rhodes of St. Louis recalls stories her mother told of her school days in the city and of meeting her future husband, Odie, "an entrepreneur and an English gentleman," famous among both teachers and students for his enterprising ways.

∼

My mother, Helen Ward, became formally aware of my dad, Odie Douglas Rutherford, when she was introduced to his bank account in her seventh grade math study of interest rates. According to my mother, on the day that they were to study interest rates, Ms. Parker, her teacher at the Lincoln Grade School, "squared her shoulders and looked heavenward" as she spoke with great pride and deliberation about how they would learn to "calculate interest rates on Odie Rutherford's bank account of $109.80, deposited at People's Bank," located on Jefferson and Market Streets.

As mother recalled, Ms. Parker explained that although he was a minor (under the age of eighteen years and requiring his father's signature for the account), Odie's bank account existed because he was an "entrepreneur," who had subcontracted with a newspaper carrier to deliver a large number (an "inordinate

Marlene Rhodes is the counseling department chair at St. Louis Community College at Forest Park, mother of four sons, and grandmother of six grand-children. (Courtesy Marlene Rhodes)

number," Ms. Parker said) of newspapers per day. Ms. Parker explained that in order to fulfill this contractual agreement, Odie organized and hired a large company of young men to deliver newspapers daily over the entire Mill Creek area, "the community in which they lived." She told the students that his business grew and thrived, and he paid his company of young men daily and saved his profits so he had opened a bank account at People's Bank.

My mother said she admired the impressive achievements of such a young "entrepreneur," especially as it was during the Depression when grown men were in soup lines and looking for work to feed their families. Men could feed their families on less than a "dollar a day," and here was a "mere boy" who had a bank account of more than a hundred dollars! Almost everyone in the community "admired and respected him," as

Helen Ward of St. Louis fell in love with a young St. Louis entrepreneur who developed a successful business while in high school. One of her favorite excursions was to go to the library. (Courtesy Marlene Rhodes)

Mom recalled Ms. Parker said. Ms. Parker reported that his parents had told the school principal of Odie's entrepreneurial spirit and the opening of his bank account.

Mom remembered that her class calculated the interest rates on Dad's account throughout seventh and eighth grades and she longed to meet him, but Ms. Parker told the class he had transferred himself to the Banneker School District to "educationally benefit" from studying with a nationally recognized educator, Dr. Sam Sheppard.

Mom graduated from grammar school and prepared to enter the ninth grade at Vashon High School in the fall term. She often thought about Odie Rutherford, "the entrepreneur," but she had no hopes of meeting him. At age thirteen she loved to swim and with other children in the community swam daily at "Bath House No. 5" on Jefferson Avenue. The children swam during the day and adults in the evening after work. During one of her daily swims with her two sisters, a great sense of excitement developed as swimmers were leaving the pool to meet a "celebrity." Someone of importance was there. She climbed out of the pool to see who it was and saw a "Nubian Prince" (words Ms. Parker had once used) basking in the adoring gaze of the children. She inquired who he was and was told he was Odie Rutherford, the man of her dreams. She described him as "tall, dark, and handsome." Since she needed a proper introduction, she begged a friend of his to introduce them.

After the introduction, she demurely withdrew as both adoring males and females surrounded him. She left the pool and returned home, but she was "smitten." She had never seen him at the pool before and assumed that this was his first and would be his only visit. When she returned the next day, however, she was "shocked" to see him swimming in deep water like a "lifeguard." She watched him and the other swimmers, and suddenly he appeared at her side and said he remembered being introduced and even remembered that her name was Helen. He was easy to talk to, and they discussed many things and gradually got acquainted that day.

She said the following day, he was waiting at the pool door when she got there, and because it was the "proper thing to do" she inquired about his family background and learned that his dad owned a small used furniture store and also a large rooming house where he rented rooms to railroad porters, who needed rooms between their trips. The Mill Creek community was near the Union Railroad Station in downtown St. Louis, so business was good. He told her that his mom worked at a tobacco company, that he had an older brother and sister. He was fifteen years old and was from England.

Mom said when he said he was from "England," she almost "swooned." She concluded that this "Nubian prince, entrepreneur, outstanding swimmer, with serious dark eyes" was also an "English gentleman." A serious courtship ensued, and they became inseparable, although always chaperoned by her two sisters. The courtship continued during the summer months with daily swims for at least a couple of hours before he went to work with his crew. Sometimes on Saturday they went to the Star or Comet Theater or roller-skated in her basement, played board games, "funny cards," and listened and laughed as her father described his customers' "crazy behaviors."

When she entered high school Odie became her math tutor, and they went to dances and school events together. When she was fifteen and a sophomore, he was seventeen and a senior, and they were "madly, crazily, and dangerously" in love as they were no longer chaperoned by her sisters. Odie proposed, and they shared their love and desire to marry with their parents.

Mom remembered both sets of parents "laughed and discounted their puppy love," told them to wait until after Mother's graduation, and assured them they had a "lifetime for marriage, babies, and responsibilities." Mom said they could not dissuade their parents, who would not allow them to discuss the subject of marriage, and when they could not convince their parents how strongly they loved each other— they took matters into their own hands and conceived me.

Mom said when they told their parents of her "delicate condition," there was a desperate cry from both families for immediate plans for a marriage. She and Odie were swiftly taken to city hall where the parents provided their permission for marriage and for blood tests to be taken. Finally the young couple enjoyed a home wedding with family and a small circle of friends.

After their marriage, Dad decided they should move into their own house. He took his savings and rented a modest rooming house. They took in roomers, an itinerant pastor and his wife and two working relatives. The roomers made it possible to pay the rent, and Dad and his crew sold many papers for additional income. Dad completed evening high school and enrolled in the Molar Barbering School, where he achieved second place on the state barbering exam. He was never hired for Molar Barbering positions, although his qualifications exceeded those of other applicants. So he

Odie Douglas Rutherford, St. Louis entrepreneur who won Helen's heart, with their son. (Courtesy Marlene Rhodes)

resolved to work for himself and eventually opened his own barbershop, a used furniture store, a confectionary, and a small dry cleaners—ever the "entrepreneur."

After my birth Dad skated to Homer Phillips Hospital every day to see us as Mom recovered in the hospital for thirty days. My birth was followed eventually by that of two siblings, my sister and brother, and my parents settled into a tumultuous life and a love affair that lasted a lifetime. But when Dad settled Mom in their first new (rooming) home, he had told her he had a confession to make. He said his family was from England, but England, *Arkansas*.

~

7

# Why We Tell Stories

Tracy Milsap, a storyteller and "story keeper" of Grandview, Missouri, who "weaves words into vivid pictures to re-create other times, other places, and other people," has written eloquently of the value of stories in modern life.

~

There are among us, a myriad of story keepers in every community and every corner of the world, collecting, remembering, and telling our stories, our legacy, our lives, story lives that surpass every difference among us—gender, culture, age, class, and persuasion—to reach us where we are on common ground, where we connect, often disconnected from our immediate and extended families, our surrounding communities, and even ourselves. We need these modern human libraries. They are preserving our existence, remembering our strengths and shortcomings, sharing our beliefs and passions, and revealing our purpose. They are the link through our traditions and everyday moments to each other, beyond our present into our future.

My maternal grandmother, though she is deceased, yet lives

Described as an artist and educator, speaker and storekeeper, Tracy Milsap eloquently tells of an important experience in her life. (Courtesy Tracy Milsap)

through my remembrance and recounting of this story. Her faith was unyielding, her expectations high, her way tough, her love real, and I am so very thankful.

"Tracy Lee!" I can still hear her calling my name—my maternal grandmother. And when my grandmother called you by your first and your middle name, you best answer. My grandmother bore seven children—two boys and five girls. She pierced every single one of those girls' ears the old-fashioned way—with a cork, a needle, and some thread. She didn't pierce the boys' ears because, well, it just wasn't acceptable back then. But, when my grandmother pierced your ears, it meant you were a "Big Girl" in the family. This was one time-honored family tradition.

My grandmother said that she lived by two books—the Holy Bible and the Farmer's Almanac. And she consulted both of them to determine just exactly when she would pierce your ears. It is exactly how she chose the day and the hour.

When my grandmother called me in that day, she was sitting where she usually sat, on the side of her bed. I sat down where I usually sat, on the stool between her legs, and she sang her favorite hymns, quoted the scriptures, and reminded me of the "do's and don'ts." Now, when Grandmother spoke, it was in your best interest to listen. See, there was bound to be some sort of test to check for good paying attention. And that day, like all other days, I did *not* want to fail one of grandmother's tests. I was so busy listening to what Grandmother was *saying* that I did not notice what she was *doing*. I was concentrating so hard on singing along, quoting my scriptures, and repeating her wise adages that I did not realize what was coming. She had kneaded my earlobes, studied my small face, threaded her needle, and placed the cork at the back of my ear before she began to pierce that ear. Oh, I knew then what she was doing. She pierced the other ear the same way.

Next, Grandmother spun me around, handed me the looking glass, studied her handiwork, and smiled. She explained that she had done her part, and now it was my turn. She said for seven days I must pull the strings around and around in my ears—morning, noon, and night. She said I wasn't going to like it because it was bound to sting and stick and puss a little, but it had to be done or my holes would close, and "Nothing worthwhile comes easy." And, if they did close, she didn't know when she'd pierce my ears again. Well, I didn't want my holes to close. I wanted to be a "Big Girl" in the family.

Grandmother was right. I didn't like it, but for seven days, morning, noon, and night, I pulled those strings. And on the eighth day, my grandmother called me again—by my first and my middle name, "Tracy Lee!" And, of course, I went right away. When I reached her room, she beckoned, studied my ear lobes, and cut the strings. She told me to fetch her straw broom, and she cut two pieces just so. She burned both ends of both pieces and placed them in my ears. And, after commending me, she repeated the instruction and warning she had given me before.

"I've done my part but your part is not done. For seven days you must turn the straw broom in both ears—morning, noon, and night. You're still not going to like it. Your ears will sting and stick and puss just a little, but it has to be done or your holes will close. And, if they do, I don't know when I'll pierce your ears again. Remember, nothing worthwhile comes easy." So for seven more days, I turned those straws—morning, noon, and night. She was right. I didn't like it, but I did it— even after they got irritated and sore and my grandmother went into her kitchen and made a poultice or a soothing salve. See, I *wanted* to be a "Big Girl" in the family.

Eight days went by, and Grandmother called me again—by my first and my middle name, "Tracy Lee!" And of course, I went right away. This time she beckoned, studied my ear lobes, pulled out the straw broom pieces, commended me, and presented me with my very first pair of golden hoop earrings. *Oh my*! I was a "Big Girl" in the family.

~

In the Coggswell family, the stories each of us tells come from our family and individual experiences. I grew up in a time and place very different from our present home in Frankford, Missouri. As a very inquisitive child (some might say "nosy"), I started learning to become a twentieth-century griot in my great-grandmother's boardinghouse in inner city Patterson, New Jersey. I learned stories my great-grandmother told me as "lessons," and I also heard stories from my great-grandfather, Uncle Pete, other family members, and various boarders, including Papa Nash, the conjurer, and Uncle Buddy, the town mourner. What adults did not tell me, I often managed to "overhear." I heard my great-grandmother Marie Wallace Cofer recount family history going back six generations. Many of her stories revolved around her own grandmother Mammy Kay, who was born into slavery.

Slave traders had captured Mammy Kay's mother and aunt in Africa. On board the ship Mammy Kay's mother saw her sister jump overboard into the ocean rather than become a slave. Her mother was taken to a plantation in Virginia but was later sold when Mammy Kay was only a child.

"Still," my great-grandmother used to say, "she did not lose heart." She often said, "In her heart Mammy Kay never was a slave, because she was too ornery." My great-grandmother told many stories about her own grandmother, who died at the age of 102 in 1939.

I guess one of the reasons I remember one story so well is because we are all fat in our family. All the women are fat. My mother is fat, my grandmother is fat, and my great-grandmother was fat. My great-grandmother used to always tell us, "Now don't worry 'bout that none 'cause that's the way you all supposed to be." And the reason we were supposed to be fat was because her grandmother Mammy Kay "almost lost her life for a biscuit."

∼

It seems that Mammy Kay had gone into the kitchen of the owners' house. The owners had taken her into the house to work after her mother was sold and her father had run away to look for her. Some of the other slave children were able to get extra things to eat because they had, some of them, a mother and a father who could bring them extras. But Mammy Kay didn't have anyone now and couldn't get extras, and when she was in the kitchen she saw a biscuit. She knew she wasn't supposed to have the biscuit, but she was hungry. And that biscuit would be a rare treat, a luxury to say the least.

Well Mammy Kay ate that biscuit and the mistress came in the kitchen and "whacked her upside the head," my great-grandmother said. "See, now, Mammy Kay was just like the rest of us, she had a temper, had a bad temper. So she started a fightin' with the mistress. You know, in those days, you wasn't supposed to fight with no white woman, no white man, nothin' white, so Mammy Kay had to get outta there. And she ran."

From my great-grandmother I learned that, like many slaves, Mammy Kay found refuge in a Native American community, where she raised three children and learned the art of trapping. She earned money for her family by selling the skins of animals that she trapped to buy calico cloth to make dresses to sell. She and one of her daughters were later kidnapped and sold back into slavery, before emancipation finally freed them for good, my great-grandmother said.

∽

My husband, Truman, tells stories he learned from his Native American family about the time before recorded history, when the First People lived in the land. His stories have been told for centuries and are now retold in Missouri. He remembers legends he learned about a time long ago.

∽

When we reached our early adolescent years our elders sat us down outdoors early in the evenings during the fall season, when the sun was still on its westward journey, to listen to the aged storytellers tell of the "Ice Giants and the Ice Children," who ruled the world way back in that time that no one remembers. They said an Indian shaman first related the story to the Indian people of the northeastern United States when he was 170 years old. We listened and wondered.

The aged storytellers told of the time during "The Moon of the Falling Leaf," when Father Sun began his long journey to visit Grandfather Sky, who lived in his sky wigwam on the other side of the sky. Grandfather Sky was very, very old, and his fires were almost burned out. All the people gathered outside at daybreak on that day and looked upward at the sky and saw Father Sun become smaller and smaller until they could no longer see him. The sky became darker and darker, and the people felt a breeze come over them. The breeze became cooler and cooler. Suddenly they saw a "Great Bird" on the horizon moving slowly as if gliding toward them. It had a wingspan that stretched from one side of the day to the other.

When Great Bird reached the people, he told them, "Be not afraid, for I have a message from Father Sun. He said tell all my little children that I will return one day."

Great Bird plucked the largest feathers from his wings. The feathers drifted down among the people, and Great Bird instructed the people to get on the feathers that had fallen. Then Great Bird flapped his wings, and the feathers quickly blew across the great waters and landed on the Winnuppee Islands. There the people heard a loud eerie noise coming from their homelands across the great waters. With a growing sense of fear the people looked toward their homelands and saw the great swirls of ice and snow, destroying everything in sight. It was then that the people knew it was the Ice Giants and Ice Children, who lived very far away in their ice wigwams in the North Country.

As the people looked toward their homelands, they saw the trees on the Winnuppee Islands start to fall to the ground and splinter. The ground they were standing on began to shake and tremble, then it slid into the great river. To their surprise the people realized they were standing on the backs of the "Giant Turtles," but the little Muskrats, who were swimming nearby, came to their rescue and told the people to go underneath the Great Turtles' shells.

"There you will be safe on your journey to the bottom of the great river. Once there, we will search for the path to Mother Earth's abode at the center of the earth."

Once the little Muskrats located the right path, the people began their long journey to the Center of the Earth and to Mother Earth's Abode. The path was dark, damp, and narrow, and no one knew how long it took the people to reach the end of the path that led to the center of the earth.

At this point, as we listened to the story, the sky was becoming quite dark and the temperature was dropping, so some of the elders started a fire to keep us warm as the aged storyteller continued his story. As the people came to the end of the dark narrow path, he said, they "entered into a great opening and were able to see more clearly." They saw a large black crow flying about and squawking loudly as if having a terrible fit, and then abruptly it became silent and still.

The people began to look around but saw nothing until a warm feeling came over them, and the voice said, "Be not afraid, my children. Here you will stay until Father Sun returns from his journey to the other side of the sky."

The people knew it was Mother Earth speaking to them. No one remembers how long the people stayed in the great opening with Mother Earth, but one day they heard a sound like gurgling water and saw light seeping through the great opening.

Then Mother Earth spoke to the people, saying very graciously, "Father Sun has returned from his long journey to the other side of the sky and wants to see his little children."

So the people left Mother Earth's abode and returned the same way they had come. They walked through the dark narrow path and met the little Muskrats that guided the Great Turtles, with the people under their shells, to the top of the great waters.

Once there the people heard songbirds singing their beautiful songs, and as they came out from beneath Great Turtles' shells, they saw grass and plants growing on the Great Turtles' backs, and when the people looked up to the sky they felt soft southerly breezes touching their faces. Then they looked toward their homelands and saw that the great swirls of ice and snow were still there, but suddenly they noticed bright sun rays break through the clouds above and descend downward. As the people watched, they saw the great power of Father Sun begin to chase the Ice Giants and Ice Children back to the ice wigwams they had come from. But some of the Ice Giants stumbled and fell, and the spots where they fell became the larger lakes and rivers; some of the Ice Children fell, and the spots where they fell became smaller lakes and rivers. And ever since that day we have had the Moon of the Falling Leaf, the Moon of the Snowshoes, the Moon of Planting, and the Moon of Hot Suns.

～

And that was the end of the story of the Ice Giants and Ice Children that Truman told.

My great-grandfather Uncle Pete, who used to talk about Missouri, often told stories of the natural world around us. According to him, he could communicate with animals. And every animal or insect or bird he ever came into contact with had special powers. He believed that every animal was to be respected and loved. It was a lesson our own son, Truman Jr., took to heart, and in Frankford when he was about eight years old he learned and told the story of "Chuck, the Elusive Buck," set in northeast Missouri in the twentieth century but reflecting beliefs going back to the time when animals talked.

~

No one knew exactly how old Chuck, the northeast Missouri buck, was, but hunters from far and near had tried for many years to kill him. Young boys who had hunted with their fathers and were now men could still remember their fathers' stories about how Chuck had gotten away. Large sums of money had been offered and big bets had been made, but to this day, no one had met the challenge of killing Chuck.

When hunters first started trying to get Chuck, some twenty years or more ago, there were stories that the buck would let the hunter get very close to him. Then, just when one of them thought he had a good aim on Chuck, the buck would disappear, and "from somewhere in the distance he would let out a loud chuckling noise." Someone named him the Chuckling Buck, which was later changed to Chuck the Buck, and the name stuck.

Some of the hunters said that they had been close enough to touch Chuck. They said he had a ten-point rack on his head. Others said he had antlers like an elk and he stood seven feet high. Some even vowed that Chuck was a ghost, and they had seen him fly. There were many stories told by the hunters, who refused to believe that a wild animal could possibly outsmart them.

Chuck, who lived near Hannibal, Missouri, had stories of

The Coggswells—Truman, Gladys, and Truman Jr.—on the Mark Twain Riverboat in 1992. (Coggswell Collection)

Truman Jr. became well-known in northeast Missouri for his storytelling skills. (Book cover)

his own to tell, and when hunting season was over he and his friends who had survived the hunters' bullets that year would exchange stories about how they got away. They all thought that hunters were a strange bunch of animals. They got the biggest laugh when they talked about the hunters who sometimes got so frightened they would shoot at the slightest sound, which, of course, only warned the animals that hunting season was on.

Chuck liked to tell the story of the time when he came closest to getting killed. One winter, while he and his two sons were strolling through the woods looking for food, they noticed a hunter had fallen asleep by a tree, only a few yards from where they were standing. He had probably been waiting to shoot a nice big buck.

"That man is going to freeze to death if he doesn't wake up soon," Chuck said to his sons.

"Better him than us," one said.

"That's right. He sure wouldn't care about us if he was awake, so why should we care about him?" the other asked.

Ignoring his sons' warnings, even though he knew they were right, Chuck told them to go three miles north and wait for him at the river.

They didn't want to go, but they had a deep sense of respect for their father and they always obeyed him. They were also very smart young bucks and knew it would not be wise to argue with the buck whose reputation made everyone look up to him. Their father was a legend in the woods as well as in the homes of hunters who wanted his head to hang in their living rooms as a souvenir.

When his sons were out of sight, Chuck eased over to where the man was sleeping and nudged him. The man woke with a start and almost jumped out of his skin. When he looked around to see what had touched him, he saw the huge buck gallantly striding away. He knew right away that it was Chuck. He reached for his rifle and aimed. When his scope showed he had a clear shot, he fired.

The man was so excited, he could barely catch his breath, but when he did, he ran over to the place where the buck should have fallen. When he got there, there was no sign of Chuck. Minutes later Chuck arrived at the lake where his sons were waiting. When they saw him, they were horrified. Chuck's side was bleeding. When Chuck saw the worried look on their faces, he smiled and told them not to worry. The bullet had only grazed his side. His sons were relieved, but they could never understand why their father would risk his life to save a hunter.

"That is not important," Chuck told his sons. "The important thing is that, once again, I have escaped the hunters and, most likely, given another one a story to tell."

∽

Stories are entertainment, but they can also be history, life lessons, oral literature, and myth. A story that has made the rounds in storytelling circles tells of a group of philanthropists who wanted to improve the lives of Africans and believed one way to do so was to provide televisions for the villagers to watch and learn from. The Africans accepted the televisions and watched in awe as images from other countries graced the screen. With a sense of pride and accomplishment, the philanthropists left the Africans to their new form of education, knowing that enlightenment for them was just around the corner.

When they returned six months later, they found the televisions dusty and unused. Disappointed, they questioned the Africans about their neglected televisions.

"Your television has stories that you know, but we have a live storyteller, and he knows us," one replied.

Our storytellers and story keepers know us, our history, our beliefs, our literature and myth, and through their stories they share with us the life lessons they have learned. Some of the stories have lived for centuries, and if we hand them down, they will live for centuries more to come. That is why we tell stories.

# 8

# Change and Continuity in
# Missouri Storytelling

When my great-grandmother and great-grandfather told me stories, I always thought the stories were theirs alone, perhaps created on the spot and told just for my benefit. Every story always seemed to exactly fit the occasion or event that inspired it. Later I learned that other adults sometimes knew the same stories but did not always have the exact information that my great-grandparents had. Still later, I realized that stories travel from person to person and place to place, changing to fit the circumstance and environment. But I was still surprised to learn when I came to Missouri that one of my great-grandfather's stories had been told in western Missouri more than a century earlier.

Mary Alicia Owen was born in St. Joseph, Missouri, in 1850 and became fascinated with the stories she heard as a child from the African Americans in her hometown. Visiting their homes whenever she could, she listened as they shared stories with one another, and she often begged to have more stories from them. In the late 1880s, Owen read a book by Charles Godfrey Leland, *Algonquin Legends of New England*, which had been published in 1884.

Recognizing that the stories were similar to some she had heard as a child, she wrote Leland and, as he had requested in his book, sent

**HE CAUGHT HER BY HER LONG, FLOWING HAIR.**

The Eagle Who Wanted to Become a Girl. (Drawing by Juliette Owen; courtesy State Historical Society of Missouri, Columbia)

him a few of the stories she knew. He urged her to attend the first International Folklore Congress in London in 1891. She decided to go and gave a talk about stories she had collected. Her talk received an enthusiastic response, and at Leland's suggestion she prepared a collection of the stories for publication. When her book was published in both London and New York in 1893, it gained international praise.

Owen's stories echo both African and Native American themes, reflecting the cultural heritage of the population along the Missouri River, where several Native American tribes lived and hunted until the Platte Purchase of 1837 took away their hunting grounds and forced them farther west into Kansas and Iowa. Owen learned the story of "The Eagle Who Became a Girl" from one of several residents of St. Joseph who often told her stories, Madame Angelique Bougareau, called "Big Angy" by her friends. Madame Bougareau said her father was a great French hunter and her mother was "chile to der big chief of the Iowas." The Ioway Indians had lived in a settlement near St. Joseph until they moved to Kansas and Iowa.

The story Mary Alicia Owen collected differs somewhat from the one my Uncle Pete told my great-grandmother and she told me, but "The Eagle Who Became a Girl" is clearly the same story as "Why the Eagle Has a Bald Head." The Owen story takes place on the Missouri rather than the Mississippi River, and Big Angy's version goes like this.

∽

In the old times, the great Thunder-Bird and his children lived on a high bluff. One of these children would not mate with another eagle. The reason was that she had, while sailing through the sky, seen a handsome young man sitting on the bank of the Missouri, the "Big Muddy" river, and watching for the great channel catfish which once every summer comes to the surface and talks and prophesies. From that moment the eagle loved the man, though she knew he could not fly, but must always creep along the ground. For a long time she was ashamed to speak, but when she saw him with a girl, she could not endure it, and went to her father and asked him to bring to her the young man. This could not be, and her father, very angry at her foolishness, told her so. She entreated so vehemently that he finally said she might go among men, but then could not set foot in Thunder-Land. She agreed to go, and he changed her into a girl—all but her feet, they remained eagle's claws, all his sorcery could not make them different.

"Let no human eye see your feet," he said, "or you will again become an eagle."

She heeded his words. She went among the people, she won the love of him she came after, she went to his house and was happy for a little while, only for a little while, for soon he began to wonder why his beautiful wife never took off her moccasins and leggings. For a time he said nothing, but after he saw her go through a stream and come out dry-shod, he was troubled, and tried to make her show her feet. He could not tell whether he had married a witch or a woman under an enchantment.

When she would not take off her moccasins, he resolved to find out why, so he watched her until she fell asleep and then cut a hole in one of them. He saw the dreadful claw. At the same moment she awakened, she looked at him with the fierce eyes of an eagle, she sprang up, her arms became flapping wings, and, as a storm struck the lodge and scattered its poles and painted skins, she rose in the air. He caught her by her long flowing hair, but it came off in his hands, and she flew out of sight. Since then, no eagle has ever married a man or regarded him as anything but an enemy.

~

Other St. Joseph storytellers had heard different versions of the story. In the version of the story Granny told, the eagle that became a girl came to earth in a raindrop. When the raindrop broke open the girl jumped out. She told her husband "plain," Granny said, that she could not go out when the sun or the moon was shining. He agreed she should go out only when it was cloudy, but after a while he forgot, and once when he was tired after coming home from hunting, he made her go out to get the game he had flung under a tree.

She did not want to go, but he made her, and as she got the turkey and deer meat and started back, the moon came out just as she got to the door. The man saw her sail up in the air like an eagle. Granny said the girl's shoe dropped off, a bead shoe, and where it dropped, a flower grew. They call it the moccasin flower.

Blue jays, woodpeckers, rattlesnakes, and "Ole Rabbit," the Trickster, populate the stories told in St. Joseph in the late nineteenth century, and birds and animals often make an appearance in stories told in Missouri's African American communities today. This collection of stories, shared by some of Missouri's most gifted storytellers and story keepers, demonstrates the creativity that has led to continuation and meaningful change in an age-old traditional art. With the life stories shared, they provide new insight into the rich cultural lives of African Americans in Missouri during the last half-century.

# Epilogue

In her account of her experiences growing up in the Missouri Bootheel, Evelyn Pulliam said that she believes things are changing for the better. Perhaps she is right. The better is that most people in the 2008 presidential election did not vote for someone because of the color of his skin. On November 4, 2008, Democrat Barack Obama was elected the first African American president of the United States. He was sworn in on January 20, 2009. It was the largest inauguration in American history. Over a million people attended, and according to news reports, there was not one arrest.

There were many tears shed of joy and disbelief that this could happen during our lifetime. On January 30, 2009, another African American, Lieutenant Governor Michael Steele of the state of Maryland, was elected the chairperson of the Republican Party, the first African American to hold such a position.

Both men have made history. Our economy is in the worst condition since the Great Depression. Will Obama meet the challenge facing him? History will tell the story.

Although we have yet to elect a woman president, anything is now possible.

Gladys Caines Coggswell
February 2009

# For More Reading

*"A Handful of Dinky": African American Storytelling in Missouri*, by Dana Everts-Boehm (Columbia: University of Missouri Press, 1992).

*Hoecakes, Hambone, and All That Jazz*, by Rose Nolen (Columbia: University of Missouri Press, 2003). This book discusses many traditions and practices in African American communities from earliest settlement until the present day.

*Missouri's Black Heritage*, revised edition by Lorenzo Greene, Gary R. Kremer, and Antonio F. Holland (Columbia: University of Missouri Press, 1993). Originally published in 1980, this book provides a detailed and readable account of African American history in Missouri.

*Mules and Men*, by Zora Neale Hurston. First published in 1935, this is now available in a 1969 edition published by Negro Universities Press in New York.

*The Negro Traditions*, by Thomas Talley, edited and with an introduction by Charles K. Wolfe and Laura C. Jarmon (Knoxville: University of Tennessee Press, 1993). Collected by Professor Talley in the 1920s in Middle Tennessee, this extensive collection of stories represents the rich oral tradition of a people forced into slavery from their homes in Africa.

"Remembering Old Frankford," by Mrs. J. H. Lowry, in *Pike County, Missouri: People, Places, and Pikers*, compiled and edited by

Karen Schwadron for the Pike County Historical Society (Marceline, Missouri: Walsworth Publishing, 1981).

*Sayin' Somethin': Stories from the National Association of Black Storytellers,* edited by Linda Goss, Dylan Pritchett, and Caroliese Frink Reed, introduction by Eleanora Tate (Kearney, Nebraska: National Association of Black Storytellers, 2006). Gladys Coggswell is among the storytellers represented in the collection. Check the Web site at nabsinc.org.

*Voodoo Tales as Told among the Negroes of the Southwest,* edited by Mary Alicia Owen with an introduction by Charles Godfrey Leland, illustrated by Juliette A. Owen and Louis Wain (New York: G. D. Putnam and Sons, 1893).

# Index

Choir Day in, 18–22; "Chuck,
the Elusive Buck" story from,
122–25; history of, 17–18,
21–22; integration of school in,
24; Truman and Gladys moving
to, 16–17
Frankford Choir, *19*
*From Missouri* (Snow), 75–76

Gardener, Garrison, 18
Gardener, Icey, 56–57
Gardener, Nancy, 18
Ghosts, in funeral home, 42–44
Gossip, in "The Sun and the Moon,"
7–8
Gray, Jeff, Sr., 67
Gray, Johnny Vincent, 66–72
Gray, Thomizene "Dear Dear,"
67–68, 70
Great Migration, out of the South,
55
Green, Bernice Lillian, 59
Green, Roy, 58–63
Grice, Mildred, 57–58
Griffin, Fannie, 31
Grimmett, Betty, 48
Grimmett, Brenda, 53
Grimmett, Curtis, 48
Grimmett, Dawn, 52–53
Grimmett, Forrest, 48
Grimmett, Frances, 47
Grimmett, Frank, 48
Grimmett, Jerry, 48–49
Grimmett, Margaret Hendricks, 52
Grimmett, William "Jerry," *53;*
family of, 52–53; stories of,
47–53
Griots (storytellers), 14, 117

Handcox, John "Sharecropper
Troubadour," 74–77, *76*
"Handful of Dinky," 24–26
"A Handful of Dinky" (Everts-
Boehm), 14
Hannibal, Missouri, 17; African
Americans left out of histories
of, 29; black high school in,
25–26; funeral home in, 42–44;
McElroy hot tamales from,
37–38
Hawkins, Mrs., 23
Hill, William Berry, 10–11
Hill-Coggswell, Mary Francis,
11–12
History: African American ignored
in, 29, 45–46; communities'
passed on through stories,
21–22, 24, 29–30, 79–86, 98;
families' passed on through
stories, 22–23, 40–44, 48–52,
56–57, 66–71, 91–98, 106–13;
passed on through stories, 26
Holland, Antonio, 28
Howard, Hattie, 59

"Ice Giants and the Ice Children,"
119–22
"I'd Be just like Old Mose" story, 35
Illinois, slaves crossing to, 46–47
Illinois Association of Colored
Women's Clubs (IACWC),
31–32
Indians, 118; legends of, 119–22,
126–28; in Truman's heritage,
9–12, 119–22
Influenza epidemic, 56–57
Integration, of schools, 24, 67–69,
87–88

# About the Author

Gladys Coggswell at the State Historical Society Meeting in 1999, when she received the Brownlee Award. (Courtesy State Historical Society of Missouri, Columbia)

A master storyteller with the Missouri Folk Arts Program, Gladys Caines Coggswell was the first black president of the Missouri Folklore Society and is founder of the By Word of Mouth Storytelling Guild. In 2005 she received the Missouri Arts Award for her work in encouraging and preserving the African American storytelling tradition. She lives in Frankford, Missouri. She is married to artist and storyteller Truman H. Coggswell and has two stepdaughters, Donna M. Coggswell-Rymer, a certified registered surgical nurse in Edison, New Jersey, and Robin G. Coggswell, a criminal defense lawyer in Rex, Georgia. Their son, Truman Coggswell, Jr., lives in Springfield, Missouri.